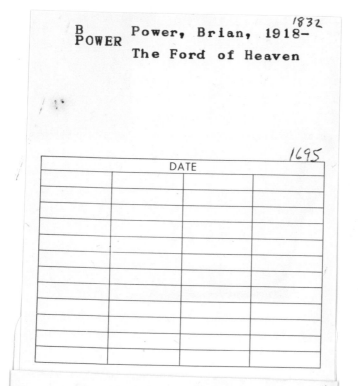

THE FORD OF HEAVEN

BRIAN POWER

The Ford of Heaven

MICHAEL KESEND PUBLISHING, LTD.
New York

First Publication 1984
© Brian Power 1984

Library of Congress Cataloging in Publication Data

Power, Brian.
  The Ford of Heaven = [Tien-chin]

  Parallel title in Chinese characters.
  1. Power, Brian—Biography—Youth. 2. Authors,
Irish—20th century—Biography. 3. China—Description
and travel—1901-1949. I. Title. II. Title: Tien-chin.
PR6066.097Z464 1984   823'.914 [B]   84-20147
ISBN 0-935576-10-X

For Prunella

'Fords and bridges are important in life. That is why in China we build our bridges with the most beautiful stone. But the Ford of Heaven, that is the most important crossing of all.'

A monk of Shanhaikwan

CONTENTS

ILLUSTRATIONS

Illustration no. 10 is reproduced by courtesy of the BBC Hulton Picture Library; illustration no. 18 by courtesy of the Royal Geographical Society.

ACKNOWLEDGEMENTS

I wish to express my gratitude to my wife Prunella, who has lived with this book in laughter and in tears from its beginnings; to the late Marjorie Villiers for her warm encouragement; to Innes Herdan for her Chinese translations; to Iona Macdonald for cheerfully typing the manuscript; to Rivers Scott for his many helpful suggestions; and to Dan Franklin for his most sensitive editing.

B.P.

INTRODUCTION

In northern China the Sea River flows through a town on its way to the Yellow Sea. Once this town had been on the coast and the waves of the sea had surged up to its oldest building, a lighthouse. But over the years the sea had retreated. By the late nineteenth century, when the decadent Manchu dynasty was nearing its end, the sea had withdrawn forty miles to the east, leaving behind a plain of mudflats and salt marshes. Through that plain the Sea River twists and turns like a serpent in search of its old lair.

Many waterways meet at the stranded inland port. Three tributaries of the Sea River, heavy with silt after descending from the high plateaux of the Interior, converge here. Here, too, the Grand Canal, built by the Tang emperors before 800 AD, ends its long journey. For dynasty after dynasty the barges carried the imperial grain tax along that artery from the distant paddy-fields of southern China to the barren desert and salt marshes of the inhospitable north.

Eighty miles to the west lies the Celestial City of Peking where the emperor, the Son of Heaven, reigned. Because the old port at the meeting of the waters gave travellers a way across them to the Celestial City, it was called Tientsin, the Ford of Heaven.

A maze of narrow creeks links the Sea River and the Grand Canal with the coastal marshlands where the nomadic boat-people lived. That mist-shrouded region was also the haunt of pirates and outlaws. At times of calamity, such as drought or flood, they raided Tientsin where they plundered the granaries.

Peasant risings, usually inspired by one of the ancient secret societies, had always been a threat to Tientsin. The professional story-tellers who roamed those parts would recite the history of the famous rebellion when Chu Yuan Chang, a poor peasant who had become a beggar monk, led a peasant host against the Mongol emperor. Having

11

seized Tientsin, the rebels crossed the Sea River in 1368 and drove the imperial army from Peking. Thus ended the Mongol domination of China which reached back a hundred years to the time of Khubilai, grandson of Genghis Khan.

The victorious peasant leader became the founder of the Ming or 'Light' dynasty (a word taken from the creed of the secret society of the White Lotus which praised as virtues the 'light' elements of nature: sun and moon, quickening fire, clear water and searching wind). It was said of the first Ming emperor that he would never allow officials to come between him and his peasant subjects.

The Ming dynasty lasted for nearly three hundred years until, in 1644, a traitor let the Manchu cavalry through a gateway in the Great Wall and the alien Manchu family of the Ching usurped the imperial throne.

Unlike the Mongols who went before and the Manchus who followed, the Ming emperors were Chinese. A nostalgic loyalty to the Ming lingered on among the people of northern China. That loyalty was kept alive by the story-tellers. They had a saying that the founding of the Ming dynasty was the first springtime; there would be a second spring when the Manchus were driven out and the Ming restored.

Four hundred and fifty miles south of Tientsin flowed the Yellow River. Between 1851 and 1853 it changed course dramatically, forming a new estuary within a hundred miles of Tientsin and flooding a vast area. People took this disaster to mean that the Mandate of Heaven was about to be removed from the feeble Manchu emperor in Peking. At Tientsin rebellion was in the air. The characters 'Restore the Ming' were daubed in white on the high stone wall which defended the town. In 1860 large numbers of destitute peasants were reported to be gathering in the marshlands. One rumour warned that an attack on Tientsin would come in the first quarter of the harvest moon. But, before the peasants and their outlaw leaders could make their move, they were overtaken by another invader. The first quarter of the harvest moon had not yet begun when, belching black smoke, foreign gunboats steamed up the Sea River.

After the gunboats came the traders and the missionaries. By the turn of the century foreign settlements protected by troops, those of Britain, France, Germany, Austria-Hungary, Italy, Belgium, Russia, America and Japan, were established at the Ford of Heaven. The second spring was not yet to be.

PART ONE

The Tide Flows

潮
水
流

I

The deep sound of a bell tolling filled the world and the room where I was sleeping. The bell sounded fainter and fainter and died away as I awoke. All was silent for a while. Then a long-drawn-out cry came from the street below.

'*Bai lian hua* . . .' The old man's cry rose and fell; rose again and fell. He sang with all his fire and strength and his voice, hoarse from the effort, made me shiver. He seemed to be crying for help to everyone in the world and to me. That cry is the first thing I remember in my life.

Bai lian hua, white lotus blossom they were called in English. I could picture the small white flowers lying in clusters on dark green leaves in the pedlar's basket. I tried to make the same cry as the pedlar. 'B. .B. .Bai. . .' A hand lifted the mosquito net which surrounded me. Then I saw a woman's face. Her yellow skin was pock-marked and wrinkled, and her black hair, turning grey, was brushed back and tied in a bun. '*Bai lian hua*,' Y Jieh our amah sang in a cracked voice. Laughing, I reached out my arms to her. She grasped my wrists firmly and tugged me to my feet. Her hands were hard and rough like her face.

I remember another face, my mother's white skin and red lips. As she bent to kiss me, her auburn hair would brush against my cheek. She had soft white hands and rings on her fingers which sometimes scratched you.

Unlike Y Jieh, who only spoke Chinese, my mother talked in English to my older brother Pat and me. Often she was sad and then she did not come into our bedroom, but stood in the doorway with tears in her eyes. When she was angry she would scold everyone: Pat and me, Y Jieh, Jieh-jieh, who was Y Jieh's daughter-in-law, and Sung Ge-ge our coolie. Afterwards she

15

would shut herself in her room for a long time.

Once I followed her there. She was sitting in front of an oval looking-glass combing her long hair. Her eyes stared at me from the glass as if she did not know me. I felt afraid and went away. After that I hardly ever went into her bedroom again.

Our house, made of grey brick, was in Meadows Road, which ran down to the river about four hundred yards away to the north. We could hear the sound of tugs and lighters hooting and sometimes the deeper and angrier blast of small steamers.

Only silent junks and sampans used the Grand Canal which came to an end half a mile to the south of our house. At the terminus of the canal was a stone monument inscribed with characters which said that the ancient waterway had been restored by the illustrious Emperor Khubilai Khan.

A narrow creek flowed sluggishly from the end of the Grand Canal down to the river. About a hundred yards from our back gate, the creek disappeared under an old stone bridge. I used to think the creek stopped there, but I found out later that it continued underground to the river. It was called the Yin Hsi or Hidden Creek. Like several other creeks in Tientsin, it had been covered over when the foreign settlements were built.

Between the Hidden Creek and our house was a stretch of wasteland littered with heaps of rubble around which grew dry, yellow grass and nettles. Chinese children played games there and stray dogs would prowl about.

In the middle of our small front garden was a tree which we called the umbrella tree because its branches hung down in a circle. A grey brick wall five feet high ran round the garden. It had gaps in the top like the parapet of a fort.

Facing us across Meadows Road was a house just like ours, except that it had a balcony with a flag-pole over its front door. It was the British Army Officers' Mess and officers in khaki uniforms and shining leather belts with swords at their sides came and went in rickshaws. Their soldiers lived in barracks at the end of the road.

At first the soldiers were Indian Sikhs who wore turbans, but in 1923 the Loyal East Lancashire Regiment came from England to guard the British in Tientsin. When the Loyals marched up Meadows Road after a parade, they would halt at the Officers' Mess, carry the Union Jack and the regimental flag inside for safe keeping and then march on to the barracks.

The Officers' Mess also had a wall like a parapet. Pat said that if the Mess was ever attacked by Chinese bandits, the officers could fire at the enemy through the gaps in the wall until the Loyals arrived to help. But what if the enemy attacked our house? I wondered. Perhaps the French soldiers would come to our rescue, because Grandfather d'Arc had been a hero in the French Army when they had helped the British to capture Tientsin from the Emperor of China.

A small Chinese woman often sat on the pavement outside our garden gate. She was old and blind and never spoke, but stared straight ahead as she held out a tin plate towards us. Beside her was a bundle of black clothes. My mother was frightened of the blind beggar woman. When we opened the gate to go out, my mother would call down to Y Jieh from her bedroom window, 'Tell her to go away.' But Y Jieh would walk on with us as if she had not heard. 'Come along,' she would say, 'don't be afraid.'

At the corner we came to the pedlars. They sat in a row leaning against the wall in the shade of the umbrella tree. Near them, two or three rickshaw coolies would squat by their rickshaws hoping for passengers from the Officers' Mess. The pedlars would stay for about an hour, then, separately, they would pick up the loads which they carried on the ends of bamboo shoulder-poles, and move on to other streets.

The tea pedlar had two wooden chests containing many little drawers. They were filled with tea leaves of different flavours and colours: red, green, yellow and black. You could choose the tea you wanted and the pedlar would put a spoonful of it in a bowl and fill it with boiling water from a kettle. In some of the drawers were herbs and big green leaves. When Y Jieh had a headache, she would buy a leaf and tie it tightly round her head with a piece of string.

Next to the tea pedlar sat the old flower pedlar. He was very thin and tanned by the sun. His faded blue cotton clothes were in rags and one of his bony knees showed through his torn trousers. On the ground beside him was a large basket full of richly scented white flowers on dark leaves. Chinese women liked to wear the flowers in their hair.

'*Ni gei wo chang chang*. . . . Please sing for me,' I would plead with him. He would grin and stand up on his bare feet. Then he would tilt back his bald head and look up at the sky. '*Bai lian hua*. . . .' As he sang, the veins in his neck stood out and his whole body quivered. The wailing sound seemed to come out of the earth and through his bones. It was the most magical sound in the world. I would stand there gazing up at him in awe until Y Jieh pulled me away.

□

Every afternoon Y Jieh took us to a small square with gardens in it, near the river. It was called Victoria Park after the Queen of England. The most important buildings in the British Concession bordered this park and there were nearly always soldiers and police marching by.

On our way we had to pass the Protestant All Saints Church. It was a dark Gothic building with the look of a castle. None of my family had ever been to it because we were Catholics.

All Saints was usually locked up during the week, but on Sundays the flag of St George flew from a tall pole in the churchyard and the Loyals, armed with rifles, paraded at the morning service. From far away you could hear the whole congregation singing hymns which sounded like hearty marching songs.

Mostly British families and the Loyals went to All Saints. Y Jieh said they followed the '*Jesu jiao* . . . the teaching of Jesus', and that our family, the Powers, had another religion, '*Tian Zhou jiao* . . . the teaching of the Lord of Heaven'. There were no words in Chinese for 'Protestant' and 'Catholic'.

Y Jieh and Jieh-jieh had no religion. Some of the servants in the other houses in Meadows Road went to the Buddhist temple in the native quarter of Tientsin at the big festivals like New Year and the August Moon Festival, but Y Jieh and Jieh-jieh never did.

I always felt glad when we left All Saints behind; it was a forbidding place, especially on weekdays when it was so dark and empty.

Beyond the church were the British Consul's house and the offices of the Kailan Mining Administration, known as the KMA, which controlled the British-owned coal-mines north of Tientsin.

We were now only two hundred yards from the river and almost at the gates of Victoria Park. Here, Taku Road, an old dirt road, cut across Meadows Road on its way from the native quarter to the estuary and mudflats of Taku. This long narrow road, which smelled of horse manure, was lined with many small Chinese shops and some warehouses called godowns. It was alive with the bustle of carts pulled by mules and donkeys and coolies swaying under the loads on their shoulder-poles.

As if the dense crowd was their natural element, people glided past each other like fish in water. But I had seen this busy street change into a deserted stretch of stones and dust with petrified men huddled together at the roadside. That was the day the outlaws were taken to the native quarter to be beheaded.

Pat and I were walking to the park with Y Jieh and Jieh-jieh when we heard police whistles and shouting. Ahead, Meadows Road was blocked by a row of British soldiers with bayonets fixed on their rifles. Policemen armed with batons were clearing Taku Road. More people arrived from behind us and we were caught up in a crowd outside the second-hand clothes shop run by an old Russian Jew.

Suddenly, everyone became silent. In the distance we could hear a drum. Nearer and nearer came the ominous sound of its beat, once every four seconds. People snatched up their children and pressed against the stalls and into doorways.

The drummer appeared, marching along the middle of the road. He wore the grey uniform of the Chinese army. His goose-step and the stiff way he raised his drumstick made him look like a mechanical toy.

Behind him, an officer rode on a dark brown Mongolian pony. Its legs were caked with dried mud. A gust of wind caught the officer's cap and he had to hold on to it with one hand to stop it blowing away.

It wasn't until the pony had passed us that we saw the prisoners. There were five of them, three men, a boy and a woman, walking one behind the other between two files of soldiers. A long rope, stretching from the officer's saddle, was tied round the neck of each prisoner, linking them together.

The leading prisoner, a tall gaunt man, stared at the crowd with wild eyes as if he was searching for someone. About two

paces behind him walked the boy. His bloodshot eyes were sunk
deep in his head. A scar ran across his cheek from nose to ear and
his lower lip was twisted in what seemed a permanent smile.

Then came the other two men and, last of all, the woman. A
piece of blue cloth covered her face, except for her eyes, which
were black. The end of the rope hung down from her neck and
trailed in the dust behind her bare feet. 'The Lotus!' someone
near us whispered. Y Jieh and Jieh-jieh looked at each other. I
felt afraid. The secret society of the White Lotus was anti-
foreign. That was all I knew. Y Jieh would never talk about it.

Once I asked the flower pedlar, but all he would say was: 'The
lotus is a flower that grows with its roots under water in the
marshlands.'

As the outlaws and their guards shuffled past, hidden now by
a cloud of dust whipped up by the wind, I was overcome by a
strange sensation. The procession I had just watched had really
been taking place many hundreds of years before. Time had
disappeared in the swirling wind, and past, present and future
were one.

More than once during my boyhood in China, I was to know
this sensation of timelessness.

□

Victoria Park was surrounded by iron railings. No Chinese were
allowed in except for amahs in charge of foreign children. The
other amahs hobbled along on bound feet, but Y Jieh's and Jieh-
jieh's feet were not bound and they walked normally. Y Jieh's
family had escaped from the cruel custom of foot-binding
because they had been water-people who lived on the move in a
sampan on the creeks and canals near the Yellow Sea coast.

Y Jieh and Jieh-jieh did not have names, only titles. Y Jieh
meant First Sister in English; Jieh-jieh meant Little Sister.

From the park gates a path led under a wooden trellis covered
with purple wistaria. In springtime swallows skimmed along the
ground and wheeled over the yellow dog-rose bushes. At the end
of the trellis near the middle of the park was a small pavilion
with a curved Chinese roof and red pillars.

On some afternoons the British army band played in the
pavilion and smartly dressed people sat on the green benches

nearby or strolled along the paths between the flower-beds. The Japanese ladies wore long kimonos and combs in the backs of their hair. When the band stopped playing for an interval, everybody clapped and the bandmaster would turn round and salute the crowd.

One day I was running past the pavilion, not looking where I was going, when I bumped into a plump lady. She was carrying a parasol which rested on her shoulder and was wearing a bright blue dress that reached down to her ankles. Her hat, which had an ostrich feather in it, and her gloves were the same blue as her dress. 'Why, it's Brian!' she said. 'Give Grandmother a kiss.' She bent down to kiss me and a strong smell of moth-balls came from her hat. I ran away as fast as I could.

Looming over the park, a dark grey building, half castle and half cathedral in appearance, commanded the centre of British Tientsin. It was called Gordon Hall after General 'Chinese' Gordon who, when he was a captain in the Royal Engineers, had surveyed and fixed the boundaries of the British Concession after Britain had won the Opium War in 1860. A high city wall had stood here. After the foreign soldiers came it was pulled down and some of its stones were used to build Gordon Hall.

Inside the hall were the police station, law court, offices of the British Municipal Council and an assembly room where concerts and public meetings were held. Outside, a crenellated battlement ran between the hall's two big towers. The arches of all the doors and windows were pointed in the Gothic style. A massive central door of wood fortified with iron bars stood at the top of a flight of stone steps leading down to the park. It was always kept closed and the only way into the hall was by the side doors at the foot of each tower.

The architect of this gloomy fortress, a Scottish missionary, had described its style as 'Victorian Tientsin'. It set the fashion and many of the early buildings in the Concession, like the Tientsin Club and All Saints Church, copied it. Most of the British settlers were agreed that Victorian Tientsin architecture was unique in the world, but Mad Mac the piano-tuner said it reminded him of a prison hospital on the outskirts of Edinburgh.

If Tientsin were ever attacked, my mother used to tell us, all the British would seek refuge in Gordon Hall just as they had done in 1900 when the Boxers, part of the White Lotus society, had besieged Peking and Tientsin. Some of the hall's windows were still bricked up and you could see the scars of that last battle on the walls.

In front of the central door, a row of old cannons on wooden trestles pointed towards the park. They were called Napoleon guns and had been presented to the British by their French allies after the capture of Tientsin. Between the cannons were some benches and on one of them Wang the fat old park policeman used to sit, rolling two walnuts together in his hand. They had become smooth and polished after many years of rubbing.

When he was in the mood, Wang would tell us tales of old Tientsin. I would sit on one of the iron cannons made warm by the hot sun and trace the big letter N on it with my finger as I listened to him. He knew a lot about the Opium War because his father had served in the Chinese Coolie Corps under the British when they and the French had bombarded and captured the emperor's four stone forts at Taku by the mouth of the Sea River before coming up the river to take Tientsin.

Every hour or so, Wang would get up from his bench to make his tour of the park. He walked very slowly and lazily as if he didn't mind what anyone was doing. But you never could tell with Wang. One moment he would be sitting contentedly on his bench like a happy old Buddha rolling his walnuts, then suddenly he would appear from behind a bush and catch you breaking a park rule. Once he arrested Pat, and I watched in dismay as Wang, marching proudly along like a soldier, led him by the arm into Gordon Hall.

Pat was always getting into trouble. He had a habit of disappearing when it was time to go home, and sometimes we were forced to leave the park without him.

As well as keeping watch over the park, Wang commanded a team of three old coolies whose task it was to drive away the crows nesting in a row of trees in Victoria Road bordering the park. The crows cawed so much in the early morning that they disturbed the residents of the Astor House Hotel across the road.

At dusk the coolies would explode a cracker under each tree in turn. The crows would fly about squawking for a few minutes before returning to their nests. By the time the coolies reached the last tree in the row, most of the crows would have settled down again for the night.

Wang pretended to be angry with his men for failing to conquer the crows, but he did not really mind for he enjoyed this evening ritual.

In a corner of the park, overlooked by the Astor House Hotel and the Tientsin Club, was the war memorial to the British who had been killed in Europe during the Great War of 1914–1918. A replica of the Cenotaph in Whitehall, London, it was surrounded by flower-beds laid out to resemble an English municipal garden.

A pagoda had once stood on this site. It was named the Light of the Sea pagoda after a lighthouse which had been here in ancient times when Tientsin was on the coast. Sometimes the gardeners working on the flower-beds turned up shells and pebbles which must have been part of the old sea-shore. How wonderful it would be, I used to think, if the waves of the sea roared and plunged right up here as they once did! And I felt sad when I realized that the sea was now far away and would never return.

A large bronze bell, all that remained of the pagoda, used to warn people that something terrible was happening, like a big fire or an attack by a war-lord. My mother told me that on the day I was born, 23 July, 1918, the bell had tolled all day long because the Sea River had overflowed its banks.

Soon after the Great War in Europe ended, the bell was taken away to make room for the cenotaph. Sometimes when playing near by, I thought I could hear the bell's distant echo and I would stand still and listen in case the sound should come back again.

Y Jieh believed that the spirits of people who used to pray in the old pagoda still haunted this corner of the park. 'Y Jieh says there is a curse on the people who took the bell away,' I told Wang one day. A look of fear came over his face. He straightened his cap, turned about and marched stiffly away. Why is he always so afraid of Y Jieh? I wondered. He shouted at the other amahs in the park, but when Y Jieh came anywhere near he would make his escape.

□

Sometimes Y Jieh had to go to the market on the way home from the park. Then we walked along Taku Road past the side entrance of Gordon Hall where the police marched in and out, until we came to the biggest godown in Tientsin. Once part of the emperor's granary, it now belonged to various merchants, but still stored the rice which came up the Grand Canal from the south of China.

Beyond the granary was the market-place. Hundreds of Chinese mingled there, talking and laughing. The stall-keepers cried out their wares and the air was thick with the smells of fresh earth on the cabbage stalks, aniseed, garlic, soya and oils of different kinds.

The high back wall of the granary formed one side of the market-place. Against this wall, the acrobats, story-tellers, magicians and conjurors performed. After Y Jieh had done her shopping we would join the audience. Next to the conjurors sat a row of men making little figures about six inches high out of different coloured clay mixed with water. The figures were called *ni ren* in Chinese, which meant 'mud men'. You could ask for anything you wished, an opera singer, dancer, mandarin or warrior. Some of the *ni ren* makers were especially good at making soldiers. They would watch the foreign soldiers parading in the streets and within minutes they could make a lifelike figure of the commanding officer. Sometimes they got into trouble with the police over their caricatures and were banned.

Once an old *ni ren* maker called out to me, '*Ying guo bing* . . . English soldier.' Then, in two minutes, he made a figure of an officer with his hands behind his back. Over his khaki uniform, the officer wore a Chinese yellow waistcoat. At this finishing touch, people near me in the crowd laughed as if they knew who the officer was. The old man handed the figure to me and I was thrilled when Y Jieh paid him two coppers and said I could keep it. The old man asked her for more money, but she said something to him and he stopped at once. Other people had long arguments when they bought things, but Y Jieh was firm and got what she wanted very quickly.

One day, when he had gone missing from the park, I saw Pat in the crowd watching the *ni ren* makers at work. He was so interested in what they were doing that he didn't notice Y Jieh and me. So this was where he always disappeared to! At home afterwards, I told him that I had found out his secret and he made me promise not to tell anyone.

□

The most exciting performers in the market-place were the story-tellers. Travelling along the Grand Canal, they would break their journey to give their recitals at the main stopping places. In the spring they would reach Tientsin. By November, when the river and the canal began to freeze, they would be on their way south again.

One of the story-tellers was known as the Fool because he spoke very little but mostly mimed his story. He came from a family who had passed down the art of reciting the ancient serial 'Outlaws of the Marshland' from father to son for several generations.

The story began with the imperial court fleeing from Genghis Khan, whose dreaded horsemen had been seen on the battlements of the Great Wall above Peking.

During the Mongol conquest a small band of outlaws made their way to a wild region of marshes south-east of Tientsin. Home of the fish eagle and the tiger, it was a remote place where few men ventured. In the heart of it was Liang Shan Po, an inaccessible mountain. There the outlaws found a perfect hide-out. Only they knew the secret way through the waters and marshes.

From their hide-out the outlaws would walk long distances to towns and villages where they helped people who were unjustly treated by corrupt mandarins, soldiers and petty officials. The outlaws went out of their way to befriend those who were usually shunned, such as former convicts, wandering monks and prostitutes.

More and more brave heroes joined the outlaws until, in the end, there were over thirty of them including two beautiful young women. They all fought brilliantly with swords and their bodies were so supple that they could twist and turn and leap high in the air to escape the enemy.

Grinning one moment and scowling the next, the Fool acted all the parts so vividly that he made you believe the story was really happening. Once, when the hero Chou San was captured and sentenced to death by a wicked mandarin, a man beside me in the crowd groaned with anguish.

Although he was lame in one leg, the Fool would leap and fall like an acrobat. He had a thick bamboo staff which he whirled and slashed about him fiercely as if it was a sword.

You could tell when he was nearing the end of a chapter, for they always ended with the heroes walking along a road, not knowing what adventures lay ahead. One day as he was finishing, the Fool prophesied that the ancient heroes would return from the marshlands and recapture Tientsin from the foreign soldiers. At this the crowd laughed and jeered, but the Fool took no notice. He bent down to pick up the coppers which people had thrown on the ground and limped away.

On my way home from the market-place, I imagined that the outlaws might steal into Tientsin that very night, such was the magic of the Fool. But as soon as I saw the columns of British soldiers marching smartly past the Officers' Mess with the sun glinting on their rifles and bayonets, the spell was broken; with a sense of relief mingled with disappointment, I realized that if they ever dared to return, the heroes of the old story would be defeated.

II

In the middle of the night my mother tiptoed past our bedroom door. She was wearing a dressing-gown which she held together with one hand at the waist. Her face was pale and sad. I slipped out of bed and followed her. On the landing she hesitated. I wished she would go back to her room, but instead she stole down the stairs.

A figure was hiding in the shadows under the staircase. I watched helplessly as my mother, who had not seen the unknown dark shape, walked on to the drawing-room. It stretched out an arm towards my mother but could not quite reach her. Then it left its hiding place and shuffled slowly along behind her. It was the small blind beggar woman!

I tried to call out to my mother to warn her, but I couldn't make a sound. She opened the door and went into the drawing-room. I heard the sound of the piano being played. The beggar woman reached the door and looked inside. Suddenly the music stopped.

I woke up shivering with fear. Many a night during the years we lived in Meadows Road I had the same nightmare, only sometimes the figure hiding under the stairs was not the beggar woman but the veiled woman prisoner I had seen in Taku Road.

My nightmare was like an illness which kept returning. I thought of telling my mother about it, but I felt too shy and kept it to myself.

□

'I should never have been forced to come here!' my mother would cry out sometimes. Then she would talk in a rambling

27

way about how she had been shipped to Tientsin when she was a child.

Her father, George d'Arc, had been one of Tientsin's early settlers. On a visit to London, he met and married Agnes O'Mahoney, a singer with the D'Oyly Carte opera company, and in 1895 returned to the north of China with his wife. They left their baby daughter Grace behind in the care of a foster mother. In 1902, my mother, who was then seven years old, was brought out to join them in Tientsin. She was their only child.

Heartbroken at leaving her home in London, and fearful of the strange couple she was now forced to live with, she became a victim of the self-pity which was to mar her life. She said very little about her parents, but she did tell us that her father was descended from the same family as Joan of Arc, and that he had served in the French Army. His wife Agnes came from a London Irish family.

My mother hated everything about Tientsin. The oppressive summers, the icy winters, the dust and the flat treeless landscape with its stagnant creeks. The hordes of coolies, surging along Taku Road like a human river, made her uneasy. But what she most feared and disliked was the apparent lack of emotion in the Chinese. She was infuriated by Y Jieh's calmness for it seemed to mock her. 'I can never tell what that woman is really thinking,' she would complain bitterly.

When my mother first arrived, the British Concession was a plot of land about a mile wide and a mile long on the south bank of the river. In this small area, British law prevailed. A gunboat, a battalion of soldiers and a police force of Indian Sikhs guarded the British community and its business houses.

Also on the south bank were the German, French and Japanese Concessions. North of the river were the Austrian, Belgian, Russian and Italian Concessions. There had once been an American Concession, but it had been made over to the British on the understanding that America could station troops there when she wished.

The foreigners in Tientsin had long lived in the anxious atmosphere of a city under siege. In 1898 there was a famine in north-east China. Roving bands of dispossessed peasants allied themselves with the secret society of the White Lotus. Some of them practised the primitive art of fighting with their bare hands. The foreigners called them Boxers. They wore bands of red cloth round their heads with the character *Fu*, Happiness, painted on them. Several of their units were composed of women.

At first the target of the Boxers' rising was the Manchu Emperor in Peking, but the astute Dowager Empress managed to divert their fury against the foreigners.

My mother used to worry about the prophecy concerning a notorious woman named Yellow Lotus. A former prostitute, she became the leader of all the Lotus members in the Tientsin area. In 1900, one of her companies besieged and nearly captured Gordon Hall. When Admiral Seymour brought reinforcements up the river and rescued the settlers, Yellow Lotus, disguised as a fisherman, escaped down the Grand Canal in a sampan. According to the prophecy, she would return to Tientsin one day, and something terrible would happen to all the foreigners.

□

On the piano in our drawing-room was a photograph of about sixty officers and men dressed in a variety of uniforms. They represented the international relief force which had served under the British Admiral Seymour against the Boxers. There were French in kepis, Germans in spiked helmets, Austrians in plumed caps, as well as British, Belgians, Americans, Russians and Japanese.

Also in the picture were one or two members of the Legion of Frontiersmen, a volunteer unit of foreign settlers who were dressed like American cowboys. How odd they looked beside the regular soldiers!

In the front row, a senior British officer lounged in his chair with studied nonchalance. Near the back of the group, a short man wearing a pince-nez and the neckerchief and wide-brimmed stetson hat of the Legion of Frontiersmen, stood on tiptoe straining to be seen. This was my grandfather. The descendant of Joan of Arc! The thought excited me and, although I did not dare to mention him because he was supposed to be my parents' enemy, I often wondered what it would be like to meet him.

I did catch a glimpse of Grandfather d'Arc once at the Bastille

Day parade in the French Park. Unlike Victoria Park, it was open to the Chinese and a big crowd gathered opposite the saluting base, a platform draped in blue, white and red with the words *Liberté, Egalité, Fraternité* displayed in big gold letters.

The French Consul sat on the platform with his guests, who included the director of the Banque de l'Indo Chine and some French priests and religious brothers in black soutanes.

The bugles and drums of the French colonial regiment of Annamites led the march-past at a brisk pace. At the rear of a long column of troops came the French veterans of the battle against the Boxers. The veterans were all out of step as they hurried to keep up with the regiment in front of them. Then I saw him! Grandfather d'Arc in his cowboy hat was leading a small group of stragglers who had become separated from their unit. Walking at a slow, deliberate pace, he seemed to be in command of his own army, who were retreating with as much dignity as possible from a far-off battlefield.

My mother said it was a tragedy that the Allies had ever fallen out. 'They used to be such good friends,' she would say. 'Crusaders! That's what Kaiser Wilhelm called them.'

The Kaiser had a dread of millions of Chinese swarming over the world. Addressing his regiments before they left Germany for China, he would tell them: 'You are going to join the crusade against the Yellow Peril.'

'The Kaiser was Queen Victoria's cousin, you know. And King Leopold of the Belgians was her nephew,' my mother would repeat, clinging to the memory of the good days when the crusaders were still united and had not yet begun to compete against each other for railway and mining rights and other concessions in China.

'The war between Russia and Japan . . . that was when we first lost face with the Chinese,' my mother said. 'It happened so soon after the Boxer Rising, too.'

Both Russia and Japan had designs on Manchuria. In 1904 a Russian fleet, blessed by the Tsar Nicholas II and his friend the German Kaiser, sailed via the Cape of Good Hope and, after a perilous journey, anchored two hundred miles from Tientsin in a gulf of the Yellow Sea.

The Russians had sailed into a trap. The Japanese Admiral Togo closed in and destroyed their fleet in a surprise attack.

Soon afterwards, like wreckage washed up from the sea, hundreds of Russian refugees reached Tientsin from Manchuria. They were the first destitute foreigners the Chinese had ever seen.

Never again were the Allies to regain that unity which their soldiers displayed so proudly in our old photograph.

□

I was in the garden one day when I heard my mother playing a solemn tune by Bach on the piano. I could tell that she was sad and I wished there was something I could do to help her. Feeling very shy, I stole into the drawing-room. She stopped playing when she noticed me and I expected to be sent away, but instead she asked me to sit down. Then with tears in her eyes, she told me her tragic secret. More than anything else in the world she had wanted to be a nun.

When she was ten years old, my mother had been sent as a boarder to the convent school of the Franciscan Missionaries of Mary at Tsingtao, a port in Shantung Province occupied by the German Army.

She learned to play the piano and, in time, became assistant organist. The soothing voices, the white habits of the nuns and the flowers on the altar in the quiet chapel were a balm after the feverish alarms of Tientsin. But she was forced to return to her parents for the holidays which she dreaded.

At that time, George d'Arc owned a stable and a pony and carriage business in Racecourse Road, not far from All Saints Church. He also built a small hotel there which was patronized by ships' officers from the steamers and tugs which came up the Sea River.

Long before the holidays were over Grace would pine for the pleasant seaside climate of Tsingtao and the convent.

When her schooling was completed, she stayed on at the convent as a music teacher giving piano lessons to the girls. In the summer of 1914, when she was nineteen years old, she wrote to tell her parents that she had decided to become a nun.

Agnes d'Arc took the next train for Tsingtao. There was a stormy scene in the convent parlour. The Mother Superior, Mother Maria della Strada, was no match for my grandmother and could only whimper, 'If it be God's will.' For the second time in her life, Grace was dragged off to the town she hated.

In August war broke out in Europe and many German families, including Grace's friends and pupils, left for Germany. Broken-hearted, she languished in her hotel prison. When her mother tried to introduce her to Mr Selby, a wealthy English estate agent, she fled from the room in tears.

To the Europeans in Tientsin, the fighting on the Western Front seemed unreal and far away. British residents still frequented Kiessling and Bader's café in Kaiser Wilhelmstrasse in the German Concession, where the orchestra played Viennese waltzes. Outside the café they mingled with the few remaining German officers and their ladies as they strolled about the tree-lined square dominated by a bronze statue of the Kaiser as a knight in armour.

When the *Peking and Tientsin Times*, an English-language paper established by Old China Hands in Tientsin, published some articles about the war, Mr Woodhead the editor received letters from British readers protesting against his anti-German tone.

Then one day the news broke that Japan had declared war on Germany and had marched unopposed into Shantung Province to seize the ports formerly occupied by the Germans. For a time there was unusual quiet at the coffee tables in Kiessling and Bader's, but Mr Woodhead assured his readers that there was no cause for alarm. Japan was an old and trusted ally of Britain. What mattered was that the Concessions should be defended against any attempt to regain them by the Chinese. Japan could be counted on to do that.

One day early in 1915, Grace was sitting in the small hotel entrance hall when a tall handsome man came in carrying a suitcase. The brass buttons on his uniform bore the imperial dragon of China. Her knight had come to the rescue.

At the Saint Patrick's Society ball held in the Astor House Hotel, Grace had eyes only for the tall young man, whose name was Stephen Power. Agnes d'Arc was quick to notice the change in her daughter; the pining convent girl had become a woman of passion. Grace danced every dance with the man who spoke with a strong Irish accent and whose ill-fitting evening suit looked as if it had been hired from the Russian old clothes shop in Taku Road.

Mr Selby, whom Agnes had thought of as a prospective son-in-law, had been completely cut out by Stephen Power. Furious at being thwarted, Agnes consulted her husband George. He had no particular liking for Mr Selby, but he had hoped that his daughter might marry a military officer and not a junior officer in the Chinese customs service.

Stephen Power was banished from the hotel. Within the week Grace fled to the house of an old school friend. As soon as possible she and Stephen were married at the Catholic Church of Notre Dame des Victoires in the French Concession. Two people attended their wedding: an Irish customs officer and Brother Faust, a Dubliner who taught at the French Marist Brothers' school.

On the piano in our drawing-room, next to the picture of the foreign soldiers, was a framed photograph of my mother and father taken on their wedding day. They were standing in front of a folding screen with Chinese flower paintings on it. My mother, in a long white dress with a veil and a wreath of flowers on her head, had taken my father's right arm which was held out stiffly. He looked like a waxwork figure on which a suit of clothes had been draped.

Sometimes when she played the piano, my mother would gaze wistfully at this photograph and I could tell that she was picturing herself as a novice about to enter a convent.

□

Agnes d'Arc never forgave her daughter Grace for marrying Stephen Power, and Grace never forgave her mother for imprisoning her in Tientsin. Like two fish in a small, murky pond who each instinctively regarded the other as a threat, they avoided any encounter as if their survival depended on it.

What skill and vigilance, what magical powers it must have taken for my grandmother and my mother not to meet in the four hundred square yards at the centre of the British Concession! Whether out walking in Victoria Park, shopping in Victoria Road, attending a reception in the Astor House Hotel or listening to a concert in Gordon Hall, they always managed to keep as far apart as possible. When I was out with my mother and she suddenly altered course and crossed the street, I knew

that not far away, perhaps only around the corner, would be the
plump figure in a feathered hat, carrying a parasol.

On Sundays my grandmother used a side chapel at Notre
Dame des Victoires, while my mother took us into the nave for
mass. Even Father Molinari the parish priest did not dare to
spoil this enmity between mother and daughter. After mass he
would take care to greet my grandmother first. Only when she
was safely in her rickshaw and on her way did he seek out my
mother.

This state of hostilities was, however, interrupted twice a
year. Both my grandmother and my mother were superstitious
about our birthdays, Pat's in July 1916 and mine in July 1918.
On each of those anniversaries there was a strict ritual.
Grandmother would come to our house with a present. She
would stay for tea and then, the truce over, she would depart,
not to be seen again until the next birthday.

'Poor mite,' I remember my grandmother saying on my
birthday as she looked at me and shook her head, 'what a time to
come into the world.' It was well-known family history that
when I was born we were marooned by flood waters in our house
in Meadows Road and Y Jieh had acted as midwife to my
mother. Meanwhile, at the other end of the world, the British
and German armies were fighting the battle of St Quentin, a
town in Picardy.

A few weeks later I was given the name St Quentin at my
christening. Brian, my first name, was pagan Irish and Father
Molinari had said that I must have a Christian name before he
could baptize me. Nobody could ever tell me anything about St
Quentin, and I used to think how lucky Pat was to have been
named after St Patrick.

On my fifth birthday I was given a set of carpenter's tools
which my father had bought for me in Shanghai. Pat and I were
inspecting them in the garden when we heard a pedlar call out,
'*Lao tai tai* . . . old mistress.' Before my grandmother's rickshaw
had pulled up outside the gate, Pat had vanished.

Grandmother had her own rickshaw coolie and a private
rickshaw with brass lamps on the sides and a bell that you could
press with your foot. She stepped out of it, lifted the veil which
covered her face, and walked into the garden followed by the
coolie carrying a huge parcel. Tongue-tied, I stood and watched

her. After months of cunning evasion, crossing of streets and changing of seats, here was the enemy herself calmly walking into our citadel!

My mother came down the front steps into the garden and we all helped to unwrap my present. It was a wooden motor-car, painted bright red. Inside was a seat, a small steering wheel and a pair of metal pedals. 'Lucky boy! Give Grandmother a kiss,' my mother said. Grandmother bent down and I kissed her soft white cheek. It smelt of Nestlé's condensed milk. 'Now you can go and play.' They went upstairs to the drawing-room, leaving me alone with my possessions.

I looked at the car for a while and then I turned to my carpenter's set. I picked up the saw. What could I saw with it? Beside me the shining red wood of the car looked inviting. I sawed it up into square pieces and stacked them in a neat pile by the heap of sawdust and the metal pedals. As I was finishing my carpentry, I looked up. My mother and grandmother were at the window watching me. Their faces were very red.

In a few moments Grandmother came down the steps in a hurry. The veil on her hat was down, hiding her face. She got into her rickshaw, rang the bell two or three times and called sharply to her coolie who was talking to a pedlar on the corner. He ran back to the rickshaw, got between the shafts and pulled her away down Meadows Road.

□

My mother often felt religious. Ever since her convent days at Tsingtao she had had a special devotion to the Blessed Virgin. In May, the month of Mary, she went to mass early every morning. At first she tried to take Pat with her, but as she could never rouse him in time she began taking me instead. I resented having to go in Pat's place. While I was getting dressed, I sometimes noticed him open one eye and then quickly shut it again when he realized I was watching him. But after a few days I came to enjoy the sensation of being about in the fresh early-morning air with few people in the streets.

We went by rickshaw to Notre Dame des Victoires in the French Concession about a mile and a half away. The rickshaw coolie ran down Meadows Road and turned into Victoria Road by the park. The purple wistaria was in full bloom and the crows were already wheeling in the sky above Gordon Hall before their daily flight to the fields outside the city.

At last we reached rue St Louis at the boundary of the British and French Concessions. We turned right. A hundred yards from the river was the church. When we got there the rickshaw coolie would be panting and coughing. He would sit on the pavement outside the iron railings and wait for us.

A paved courtyard led to a flight of wide stone steps and the big front doors of the church. On one side of the courtyard, a gate was set in a low stone wall. Beyond the gate a path wound through a small garden to the convent of the Sisters of Charity.

If we were early enough, we would see the nuns walking along the path to mass. They wore long blue skirts with bustles and large white starched hats with butterfly wings. My mother told me that their habit copied the dress worn by peasant women in Brittany.

Inside the church a few Chinese women knelt at the back. How peaceful it was compared with Sundays when the church was packed and the French colonial regiment of Annamites, little men in sun helmets, led by their band playing bugles and beating drums, paraded noisily outside.

We walked half-way up the aisle and knelt down in a pew on the right. The pews in front of us all had brass nameplates. Most of the names were French. The one at the very front bore the name of Monsieur Ledoux, the director of the Banque de l'Indo Chine.

A Chinese server in white surplice and black cassock lit two candles on the high altar. Their light flickered against the slender marble columns at the back of the altar which climbed up and up as if they were reaching to heaven. Above them was a large painting of God the Father with a white beard.

On the left of the high altar was the Chapel of the Blessed Sacrament. One of its walls carried a bronze plaque surmounted by a helmet and crossed spears. On each side of it hung a tricolour. This was the memorial to the French soldiers who had fallen in the battles of the Taku forts and the Boxer Rising.

On the right of the high altar was the Lady Chapel where the Sisters of Charity, two or three of whom were Chinese converts, usually knelt. My grandmother had her seat there with the

name d'Arc on a brass plate. Next to her seat was my grandfather's, but it was always empty. Every Sunday she would pray
that he might return one day to take his place among the
faithful.

Father Molinari said mass in dark glasses. He always wore
them because he suffered from sun blindness.

When the bell rang for the Sanctus, my mother buried her
face in her hands. I wondered if she was praying for my father
who was away in Hankow.

On the way home it was warmer and the rickshaw coolie ran
with his shirt tied round his waist. You could see the beads of
sweat trickling down his back. At our gate my mother paid him
ten cents. He then went to the tea pedlar, bought a cup of black
tea and squatted on the pavement to drink it.

On the landing outside my mother's room hung two holy
pictures: one of the Virgin Mary and one of Blessed Bernadette
Soubirous to whom Mary had appeared at Lourdes. Below the
pictures was a shelf and my mother often put a vase of flowers on
it under Our Lady's picture.

One day a new picture appeared beside the others. It was of
the 'Little Flower', St Thérèse of Lisieux, a humble and
obedient Carmelite nun whom Pope Pius XI had recently
canonized. She was dressed in a brown and white habit and
looked very pretty with pink cheeks. In her arms she cradled a
bunch of red roses and a crucifix. Underneath were printed her
words: 'After my death I will send down a shower of roses.'

From now on the vase of flowers was placed under the new
saint's picture. I wondered what Our Lady thought about this.
Was I imagining things or did she look displeased? As for poor
Bernadette, her eyes no longer shone and she was plainly
unhappy.

Neither Our Lady nor Bernadette had ever answered the
secret prayer I said every night at bedtime, so now I tried the
Little Flower. 'Saint Thérèse, please help to stop my nightmare
about my mother.' But no help came, and I went on dreaming
about the dark shape hiding under the staircase.

□

On Sunday mornings my mother played the organ at the ten

o'clock mass at Notre Dame and Pat and I sang in the choir. I
sang all the solo parts. Pat had just as good a voice as me, but my
mother found it harder to get hold of him for rehearsals. She was
delighted when people came up to her after mass and said,
'What a beautiful voice your son Brian has.' As my reputation
spread, I was asked to sing at nuptial masses as well.

The organ loft at Notre Dame was a frightening place to be. It
was dark and there were many dusty corners shrouded with
cobwebs. An old Chinese coolie pumped the organ bellows with
a heavy wooden handle. He was deaf and very vague and was
often so late in starting to pump that, when my mother began to
play, the organ would run out of air and give a squeak followed
by a painful wheeze. Father Molinari, looking sinister in his
dark glasses, would turn round at the altar and glare up at my
mother in the loft. She would retaliate by playing a long-drawn-
out piece by Schubert whom Father Molinari detested,
although she knew that he was waiting to carry on with the next
part of the mass. No amount of looks from him could hurry her
when she was in that mood.

The trouble was that my mother suspected Father Molinari of
taking my grandmother's part in our family war. The stern old
priest commanded his congregation as if they were a frontier
garrison under siege and was used to complete obedience, but he
was wary of my mother; he knew only too well that she had one
weapon against which he had no defence. She was the only
eligible organist in Tientsin.

Their duel continued after mass when Father Molinari came
to greet his flock in the courtyard. Here he was more vulnerable.

'Don't you miss the German hymns we used to sing in the old
days?' my mother would say to her friends in a voice so
penetrating that Father Molinari could hardly fail to hear.
'They were so virile, so musical.'

Outside the iron railings, the beggars would begin to wail.
Some of them had no limbs, only stumps. Others exposed their
horrible sores. People said the beggars spent all the coppers they
were given in the opium dens and that was why they looked so
starved.

The Sisters of Charity were always the last to leave the
church. All but hidden under their large white butterfly hats,
they walked in pairs to the convent gate.

One Sunday while I was waiting for my mother after mass, I watched the procession of nuns go by. The last one to pass through the convent gate stopped to close it behind her. She turned her head towards me for a moment and I saw that she was Chinese.

Her old black eyes looked through me as if they were reading my whole life. I had never seen that mask-like face before and yet it was a face I had always known.

She turned away to follow the other sisters. Suddenly a wild idea came to me. Yellow Lotus! Could it be her? She who had escaped down the Grand Canal in a sampan . . . And the woman prisoner in Taku Road?

This daring thought left me feeling dazed and I held on to one of the railings to steady myself. When I looked towards the convent again, Yellow Lotus had become one of a stream of butterflies floating along the garden path.

□

On our way home from church, as a reward for singing in the choir, we sometimes took a rickshaw to Kiessling and Bader's Viennese café in the former German Concession. In the square outside the café was a stone pedestal almost hidden by weeds. On this pedestal had once stood the statue of the Kaiser. In November 1918, when news of the Armistice in Europe reached Tientsin, there were wild celebrations. A crowd of excited British residents pulled down the statue. They dragged it to the forecourt of the Tientsin Club where, to the amazement of the Chinese onlookers, they battered the bronze knight into pieces.

Herr Kiessling, a fat man with two chins, strutted up and down inside the entrance to his café. My mother's friends were impressed when he greeted her in German and showed her to a table by the window. She gave the order in German and then began to tell everyone about her convent days in Shantung Province. 'German China, we used to call Shantung in those days', she would say.

While we sipped hot chocolate and ate pastries, a trio seated by some potted palm trees played waltzes by Strauss and Weber. The violinist and leader of the trio was Herr Schneider, a short pale-faced Austrian with a small moustache and sad, dark eyes.

He also played in the orchestra at the Empire Cinema.

When Herr Kiessling thought that his trio were taking a little too long over their interval, he would go and stand beside them with his hands behind his back and give Herr Schneider a sly look out of the corner of his eye. Herr Schneider would sigh, take up his bow, place a small cushion on his shoulder, settle his violin on it with great care and begin to tune each string in preparation for the next waltz.

As we were leaving, a Russian street musician in the square outside would serenade us on his balalaika. He had to play very quietly, otherwise one of Herr Kiessling's waiters would chase him away.

My mother said that the Russians were the most musical people in the world. A few Russian families crossed the river to the British Concession regularly, to attend the concerts in Gordon Hall. Among them, my mother told me, were princes and princesses and counts and countesses.

An old Russian officer, wearing the faded uniform of the late Tsar's army, took to walking up and down by the row of cannons in the park before the doors opened for the evening concert. As he passed his fellow exiles, the old Tsarist officer would salute each of them with careful dignity.

Wang, who did not like Russians or Siberians coming to his park, became very excited whenever he saw the old officer. 'He has his own park, what does he want here?' Wang would say.

Once, when the old officer came near the bench where Wang was sprawling, Wang turned away to face Gordon Hall as if he was trying to hide from him. Then I noticed that Wang had stopped rolling the walnuts in his hand. Instead, his fist was tightly clenched over them.

'The Russians lose every war they fight,' Wang would say with a sneer. 'They lost against the Japanese and they lost against the Bolsheviks.'

Wang knew a lot about the Bolsheviks, for he had served with the Chinese Coolie Corps on the Allied expedition to Siberia in 1918. That was when several trainloads of British, French, American, Italian and Japanese troops, together with a hundred coolies, left Tientsin to fight for the Far Eastern Republic of Siberia against the Bolsheviks who were advancing from the west.

The expedition was a disaster. In Siberia the Allies spent much of their time guarding their trains against marauding Cossacks who were supposed to be on their side.

After a few weeks of chaos, the Allies were forced to retreat. Listening to Wang's stories of the Siberian campaign, I had a feeling that something terrible had happened there which he was keeping secret. He looked old and frightened, like a man who had seen a ghost and was half afraid it might appear again.

'You should have seen the hundreds of Siberian refugees trying to board our train when we retreated,' Wang said. 'We had to kick them off the steps of our carriages. It must have taken them months to reach Tientsin, climbing over mountain passes, then coming down by carts or walking. Year after year they came. As late as 1924, stragglers were still coming here. And when they arrived, what did they find?' Wang gave a cruel chuckle. 'There, over the Russian Consul's office, was the red flag they had been escaping from.'

When they first settled in Tientsin, the refugees' tales of horror and their appeals for help to put down the Bolsheviks were listened to with sympathy. But, as the years passed, the old tune of their lament grew tiresome and they were treated with polite disdain by the other foreign residents. Most people felt that the expedition to Siberia was an adventure best forgotten.

□

In the Park one afternoon I watched a gang of coolies putting up a bamboo and paper arch. It stretched from the side of Gordon Hall across Victoria Road to a big shop. Wang told me that the arch was to celebrate the arrival of a new regiment of British soldiers. When the arch was finished, big letters in English were fixed to each side. On the side facing the railway station was the greeting 'Welcome the East Yorks'. On the other side were the words 'Farewell the Loyals'. The whole of the arch was covered with strings of small Chinese crackers.

There was much excitement the next day as British families lined the park railings and the verandah of the Astor House. All traffic in Victoria Road was stopped. Outside the entrance to Gordon Hall stood the chairman and members of the British Municipal Council and their guests, among whom were some elderly Chinese officials from the native quarter, wearing long Manchu-style gowns and skull-caps.

To get a better view, I crossed Victoria Road to watch from the side facing the park. From the direction of the station, the sound of a brass band grew louder and louder and then, to cheers from the crowd, the East Yorkshire Regiment, led by their drum major, came into sight. Now and again, the drum major, who was wearing white gauntlets, threw his big stick high into the air and then caught it as he marched along. People cried 'hooray' and clapped this spectacular feat.

Behind the drum major and the band marched the colonel, a stout man with a moustache. As he reached Gordon Hall, he roared 'Eyes right!' and dipped his sword in salute to the council members, who all took off their hats, while the Chinese guests bowed.

Inside the park railings, the old Tsarist officer was standing to attention, his hand raised to his cap in a smart salute. Behind him, a little to one side, was Wang. He was not watching the parade. Instead, his eyes were fixed furtively on the old officer as if he was vaguely remembering him from long ago.

Just then, spluttering, banging and making clouds of acrid blue smoke, the firecrackers on the arch began to explode. Their sharp noise sounded like machine-gun fire and frightened me.

The companies of soldiers passed under the arch, skirted the park and turned right into Meadows Road on their way to the barracks. As the smoke and fumes from the crackers drifted away, I saw a *ni ren* maker I knew from the market-place. He was sitting on the pavement putting the finishing touches to a figure of the new colonel. Beside him on his tray was a figure he had already made. It was the drum major with his arm proudly reaching up to catch his big stick.

On the following afternoon, Tientsin said goodbye to the Loyals, who had come to the end of their tour of duty. A big crowd turned out to watch them march past the cenotaph down Victoria Road on their way to the station while the band played 'Pack up your troubles in your old kit-bag and smile, smile, smile!'

When all was still again, I walked by the cannons in the park. Wang was sitting on his bench having a rest. He had had a busy day guarding his park against friend and foe. Seeing him picking his teeth with a twig, I could tell that he did not want to be disturbed so I left him alone.

One or two crows began to appear in the sky, returning from across the river. Soon they would be joined by the rest of their colony and they would settle in the trees bordering the road. It was nearly time for Wang to lock the park gates.

□

Long blasts from a ship's horn woke Pat and me before dawn. Each blast began with a high-pitched shriek and then fell to a mournful drone.

'It sounds like HMS *Hollyhock*,' I said.

Pat opened the window. 'All the lights are on in the Officers' Mess.'

I was just wishing that my father was at home and not away at Taku, when we heard the heavy tramp of soldiers marching down the road. I leapt out of bed and joined Pat. A company of East Yorks, wearing steel helmets and battle order, halted outside the mess. Three officers came out to join them and they all marched on towards the river.

All that day the roads leading to the river were cordoned off by the police. In the park, Wang strutted about as if he was an officer on parade. I asked him if there was any fighting going on, but he marched away without answering.

The soldiers did not return to barracks that evening. It wasn't until the next day that we found out what had happened.

By night, at low tide, pirates had boarded the Japanese steamer *Hokkaido Maru*, which was anchored off the British bund. They strangled the crewman on watch, surprised the captain and ordered him to sail five miles down-river to the mouth of a creek where they grounded the steamer.

By the time the alarm was raised, the pirates had unloaded the cargo, mainly foodstuffs, and made off with it in sampans.

Mr Woodhead, editor of the *Peking and Tientsin Times*, said that the carefully-planned raid, which had taken place under the windows of the Customs House, was not the work of ordinary river pirates. It had probably been based on inside information. He did not want to alarm his readers, but the raid was similar to one carried out ten years earlier on the SS *Cardiff* by the secret society of the White Lotus.

'Incredible as it may seem to us in modern times,' said Woodhead, 'this ancient revolutionary society is still active. We have become complacent. Security must be tightened and priority given to tracking down any members of the Lotus who may be hiding in the Concession.'

Within a month, the British Municipal Council had appointed a Watch Committee with the aim of seeking out members of the Lotus.

As usual, Woodhead had had his way, but only up to a point. He did not hold with committees and would have preferred a dynamic individual to take charge of the operation.

The chairman of the Watch Committee was Mr Peebles, a lugubrious Scottish accountant, one of that new breed of professional men who had begun to take charge of affairs in the outposts of the British Empire. Not for him the crusading spirit of the Old China Hands like Woodhead. Mr Peebles' way was cautious diplomacy and compromise. 'We must consult our American friends,' he would say when confronted by a problem.

At the first meeting of the Watch Committee Mr Peebles issued a short statement to the press in which he appealed to the community to be calm and vigilant and to report anything suspicious to the proper authority.

III

Late one evening when a big golden moon hung in the sky, a man in a cotton jacket and trousers stood in the middle of our backyard. In front of him floated his hands, poised one above the other as if they were holding an invisible globe. He was completely lost in what he was doing.

Slowly, very slowly, he began to move, his hands turning with the rotating globe. Bending his knees, he stretched out an arm with the palm of the hand facing forwards to ward off the enemy who threatened. Without any break in his slow, purposeful movements, he glided forwards, turned, retreated two paces and, crouching low, pointed his arm towards our back gate.

Sung Ge-ge our coolie was practising the T'ai Chi movement called 'Meeting a tiger half-way up the mountain'. This movement and 'The eagle spreads its wings' were two of his best. Whatever idea he was enacting and whatever pattern his steps followed, his body behaved in the same disciplined way as he performed the ancient and solemn ritual. He would breathe in deeply as his arms went upwards and forwards, and breathe out as he lowered them and turned to face in a new direction. Only when one foot was firmly planted on the ground did he begin to step off with the other. Like the slow-moving Sea River, flowing, whirling and ebbing, Sung Ge-ge glided among the shadows, facing invisible enemies.

The art of self-defence called T'ai Chi had its origins in ancient times when a hermit, Hua t'o, taught that people's health would improve if they learned to move like some creatures of the wild, tigers, deer and eagles. During the Ming dynasty, a conjuror who spent much time in the hills watching fights between snakes

45

and birds, added to the movements, showing how to face an attack from any quarter and how the weak could overcome the strong.

'Where there is T'ai Chi, the Lotus are not far away,' Wang the park policeman said one day, giving me a sly look which frightened me. 'Those Boxers learned all their tricks from the Tai Chi exercises.' I hoped Wang would never find out about Sung Ge-ge who looked so menacing in the backyard as he advanced silently, wheeled and crouched ready to spring.

Sung Ge-ge, whose name meant Brother Sung in English, was strong with square-shaped jaws. Because he nearly always had a wide grin on his face, people thought he was stupid but I was not so sure. In the summer he had his head shaved bald by the street barber. In the winter he let it grow into a black stubble about an inch long.

He had a one-string Chinese violin; it was long and thin with a small round box at the end like a banjo, and made a wailing sound when he drew the bow across it. After supper he would sometimes play it while he sang songs from Chinese operas.

From the backyard, a flight of steps led below ground to the coal cellar, the kitchen, Y Jieh's family room and the coolie's room, which was also used as a living-room by the other servants. Except for the poorer Russians and Siberians who could not afford one, most foreign families had a coolie. The wealthier households had a Number One Boy, a kind of butler, as well.

In Y Jieh's room there was a chest and a rush mat on the stone floor. Two baskets and an iron pot hung on the wall. The bed was made of bricks; four feet high and very wide, it took up much of the room. In one side of it was an oven which burned coal in the winter. The Chinese called these brick beds *kangs*. During the day, the bedding was rolled up at one end and you could sit on the *kang*. At night all Y Jieh's family slept on it, Y Jieh, her son A Chin and Jieh-jieh, who was A Chin's wife.

A Chin was about twenty years old. He was thin and pale and couldn't go to work because he was always ill, so he spent most of the day lying on his back on the *kang*. He felt better in the evenings and often went out before supper, returning late at night. This puzzled me for a long time until I discovered that he was an opium addict.

Pat and I nearly always had supper with the servants. In the winter and in bad weather we would have it in Sung Ge-ge's room. In the spring and summer we sat at a trestle table in the backyard. We usually had rice with cabbage or beans. On special occasions Y Jieh would make us bowsers. These were dumplings filled with a little minced meat, onion and garlic.

Our servants counted themselves lucky to have this food and they did not waste a grain of rice. Most northern Chinese never ate rice. Their diet was millet which had small yellow grains. The poorest people, like the rickshaw coolies on our street corner, ate gaoliang which tasted very bitter. It was a coarse millet which grew to a height of eight or nine feet near the salt marshes north of the river.

At supper Sung Ge-ge and Pat would tell us funny stories and make us all laugh. I would tell them all about the latest episode in the 'Outlaws of the Marshland' that I had heard in the market-place and Y Jieh would explain the parts of the story I had not understood.

Afterwards, I would sit beside Jieh-jieh and watch her practise writing Chinese characters. Kneeling on the ground, she would mix the stick of black ink with water on a flat inkstone, dip her brush into it and then hold the brush poised vertically over the sheet of white paper for a while before making a stroke. It was like a solemn moment in church.

Jieh-jieh showed me how each stroke that went to make up a character was taken from nature: a wave of the sea, the trunk of an old tree, a falling rock, the stem of a bamboo.

After her practice, she would let me take the brush and try some of the simpler characters like 'follow', which was pictured by two men, one behind the other; 'China', the Middle Kingdom, a field pierced down the centre by a spear; and 'good', a woman with a child in her arms.

So, from an early age, this beautiful and vivid language captured my imagination. On my walks to the Hidden Creek, especially if I was on my own, I began to see some of the characters Jieh-jieh had taught me in the twigs and leaves on the wasteland and in the patterns made by the stones on the dusty path. Sometimes, looking down at the creek from the old bridge, I could even see characters in the ripples made by the insects on the slimy water.

When it grew too dark to see properly in the backyard, Jieh-jieh would fold up her writing sheets. She never threw them away. In the dusk, bats would flit about us. Sung Ge-ge said they brought good luck, but my mother was frightened of them and she hardly ever came into the backyard.

□

From an upstairs window the sound of the piano floated down to us in the yard. My mother was playing a nocturne by her favourite composer, Chopin. I could always tell the mood she was in from the tone of her playing. The beautiful notes, now peaceful, now ominous with impending storms, enchanted me.

The music stopped. Then we heard people's voices. My mother's guests had arrived. 'A gin and lime for the Captain?' I heard her say. 'Bless you my dear. Steady now! Not too much lime.' There was hearty laughter and when it died down the Captain asked, 'Any news of Mr Power?' I couldn't catch any more because all the guests began talking at once in loud voices.

The moon had changed to a cold silver. Sung Ge-ge began to play on his violin. Frowning in an effort to remember the words, he quietly sang a song from an opera about the autumn harvest festival. '*Ba yue shi wu. . . .*' The song told of a ghost from the past who came to disturb the guests at a feast.

□

Pat and I were talking to the pedlars on our corner one day when we saw a tall man walking along Meadows Road towards us. He was carrying a suitcase. His shirt was open at the neck and his jacket was draped over one shoulder like a cape. 'Lao Da,' cried Pat, running towards him. My father! He was back! The Chinese all called him 'Lao Da', which meant 'the tall one'.

Filled with excitement, I raced after Pat. We struggled to carry the suitcase for him, but it was too heavy. Laughing, he picked it up again and we walked back to the corner. 'Lao Da, Lao Da,' the pedlars called out, greeting my father with smiles.

1   The author, aged five.

2, 3   The author's grandparents, George and Agnes d'Arc.

4   The author's parents on their wedding day.

5   Y Jieh with Brian in Victoria Park.

6   Jieh-jieh with Pat.

7   The servants: (left to right) A Chin, Y Jieh, Jieh-jieh and
    Sung Ge-ge.

8 Gordon Hall illuminated for the coronation of George VI.

9 Officers and men of the international relief force of 1900. George d'Arc is standing in front of the Chinese soldier in the centre of the back row.

He bought a small bunch of flowers for my mother and we went into the garden.

I was glad that my mother had not seen him coming down the road, because she did not like him walking about Tientsin carrying a suitcase. She felt that people would look down on him for it. 'I can never understand why you won't take a rickshaw, Stephen,' she would complain. She was sure to notice his clothes though, for his shirt was crumpled and his shoes were covered in dust.

Mr O'Donovan, the Inspector of Customs for whom my father worked, thought that he would get on better in his job if he improved his appearance. 'The IG thinks you should drop Stephen a hint,' Mr O'Donovan had once told my mother. The 'IG' was Mr O'Donovan's name for his chief, the Inspector-General of the Chinese Maritime Customs.

My father's work often took him to places like Hankow, I-Chang and Shanghai. We saw so little of him that, when he returned home, Pat and I would drag him laughing to our room.

He had brown hair and blue eyes like Pat and his cheeks would glow as he told us stories about the old times in County Clare in the west of Ireland where his home had been. Although he spoke about the ancient past in loving detail, he hardly ever said anything about Ireland in the present time.

When he had done, we would go on asking questions until my mother took him away and ordered us to bed. Even then my father would come back to our room and tell us more stories until I fell asleep listening to that other world in the far west where the Atlantic Ocean dashed against the black cliffs of County Clare.

Not far from those cliffs, by the mouth of the River Shannon, lies Querrin, a notorious haven for smugglers. The Powers who lived in a thatched cabin there had been fishermen for many generations. In the old days before the Great Famine, they shared two curraghs, long rowing-boats made of cow-hide, with the other three families at Querrin.

In springtime this small community would split up. Some of them would drive the cattle up to a ridge about twenty miles inland and wander with their beasts along the common pasture land. This nomadic life was called 'booleying'. A fiddler or a piper, more often than not a blind man or a cripple, would travel with the booleyers and keep them amused at night by their camp-fire.

In August they would return to Querrin to help with the harvest. Then winter brought its long hours of darkness and the chance of some smuggling.

What little learning the children gained in those times came from a wandering hedge-teacher who recited Celtic legends in Irish. The speaking of Irish was strictly forbidden, so during his lessons behind a hedge or in a barn, a look-out boy, who had a sharp eye and was the fastest runner, would keep watch for any English dragoons from Carrigaholt Castle a mile or so from Querrin.

It was the Powers' one claim to honour that Seamus Power, my father's great-grandfather, had been chosen as a look-out boy.

During the Great Famine, which began in 1845, the cattle and the fishing tackle were exchanged for a few sacks of meal. So, at last, the old way of life came to an end. What little my father said about West Clare after the famine, he said abruptly and without interest, as if he felt the magic had gone out of Ireland.

Somehow, the Powers survived. Thomas Power, my grandfather, became a roving thatcher who only returned home at harvest time. He and his wife Margaret had fifteen children, of whom three died in early childhood. Stephen, my father, who was born in 1887, was the twelfth child. From the age of ten his task was to take the ass and cart to a bog about ten miles inland, and fetch a load of peat.

As the children grew up, they left home in search of work. One went to Dublin, three emigrated to America, three joined the Royal Navy, three girls became nuns and one, Anne, stayed at Querrin to help her parents on the land.

Stephen was the last to go. In 1907 a seaman of West Clare returned from a voyage to China. He spoke of the opportunities for young Irishmen in the Imperial Chinese Customs of which Sir Robert Hart, an Irishman himself, was Inspector-General. Stephen and a few other Clare men applied for jobs in China through the Customs House in Dublin. They were accepted within the year. To save money, they arranged to work their passage from Cork to Shanghai.

Whenever I tried to picture my father's home by the Shannon estuary, I saw blue-and-grey rock, blackening seaweed and two derelict boats of withering cow-hide. Only here and there did a touch of yellow and green soften that harsh landscape. Brother Faust, our Dublin friend, was fond of speaking of Ireland as 'the Emerald Isle'. The words made me think of a place with the hardness of stone.

□

After a journey lasting eight weeks, the steamer carrying my father and his companions reached Shanghai at the end of November 1908.

Earlier that month, the Emperor Kuang Hsu had died, followed on the next day by the Dowager Empress herself. For fifty years she had dominated the Celestial City, gaining a little more time for the doomed Manchu dynasty of the Ching. In accordance with her wishes, Pu Yi, a three-year-old boy, was placed on the Dragon Throne, while his father, Prince Ch'un, was made regent.

So it was in the service of the boy emperor that Stephen Power began his work as an imperial tax collector.

The Chinese customs service collected taxes on everything that was exported and imported at the river and sea ports. By treaty, Britain administered the service, and the Inspector-General Sir Robert Hart had built it up into the most efficient concern in China. He served two masters, the Chinese emperor and the British government, for much of the money collected in customs dues went to pay off the huge sum which Britain and other foreign powers had demanded from China by way of indemnity after the defeat of the Boxer Rising.

When Stephen Power met him, Sir Robert Hart was a portly man with a white beard and side-whiskers, always immaculately dressed in a black frock-coat, white collar and cravat. A native of Belfast, he preferred to recruit Irishmen. He took a personal interest in each of them and boasted that he could recruit a man from the bogs of Ireland and, in next to no time, turn him into a smartly dressed officer fit to serve an emperor. He did not know the bogs of West Clare.

Sir Robert Hart had arrived in China in 1854. He died there
in 1911, the year that the Manchu dynasty was destined to come
to an end.

During his fifty-seven years in China he took but one brief
holiday, a visit of two weeks in Ireland. He was the most eminent
of the Old China Hands, that rare breed of men from Britain
who combined missionary zeal with an astute business sense. In
everything he did and said, he betrayed an unwavering sense of
superiority. After the Opium War and the capture of Tientsin in
1860, he was chosen by the merchants to present an address to
the victorious Lord Elgin. He ended it with these words: 'Your
great deeds and our future work will extend among the people of
China the elevating influences of a higher civilization.'

□

Heaven, having waited graciously for the Dowager Empress to
die, finally withdrew its mandate from the Ching dynasty. In the
autumn of 1911 there was drought and crop failure in central
China. Troops of the Imperial Army were in open revolt in
several provinces.

The southerner and idealist Dr Sun Yat Sen arrived in Peking
to form an uneasy alliance with Yuan Shi Kai, a war-lord who
had been the favourite general of the late Dowager Empress.

In February 1912 a republic was proclaimed and the boy
Emperor Pu Yi was forced to abdicate the Dragon Throne. He
was treated with the greatest respect. Articles were drawn up
providing for the favourable treatment of 'The Great Ching
Emperor' which gave him four million dollars a year and
allowed him to live in the Summer Palace surrounded by his
bodyguard and a retinue of concubines and eunuchs.

Uncertain about their future in Peking, some members of the
imperial family, including Prince Ching, deserted Pu Yi and
found refuge in the foreign concessions in Tientsin.

Yuan Shi Kai soon broke his pact with Sun Yat Sen and
began to rule the north of China as a dictator. Some foreign
powers, impressed by his strong government, lent him money.
Coins were issued bearing his image. Flanked by his generals in
uniforms of blue and gold, he even gave audiences in a throne
room at the Forbidden Palace. It seemed that nothing could

prevent the former servant of the Dowager Empress from becoming emperor.

Then, when he was about to be proclaimed Son of Heaven, Yuan Shi Kai died suddenly, 'made ill by shame and anger'. That was the official cause of death published in the papers, but Wang the park policeman used to tell another story of the dictator's death which was horrible to listen to.

In the weeks before the late Emperor Kuang Hsu (the one before Pu Yi) died, he believed he was being poisoned by the Dowager Empress. At night he was kept awake by the sound of her whispering and chuckling behind the silk hangings draped around his bed. Frantic with fear, he would tear down the hangings, but all he could see were bare walls.

Yuan Shi Kai had had the audacity to sleep in that same bedroom on the eve of his enthronement. Early the next morning, his aides found him dead. His face was still convulsed with terror. One of his hands clutched the silk hangings which surrounded him.

Wang would shriek with laughter when he reached the end, but I noticed that his eyes had a frightened look in them, as if he believed his own story.

□

Mad Mac was my father's best friend. I first met him when he came to our house to tune the piano. He was short and wiry, with blue eyes. His skin was freckled and his head was bald except for a fringe of red hair about his ears.

When he was young his family had been evicted from their croft in the Western Highlands of Scotland. They were sent by steamer to Australia. From there Mad Mac made his way to the west coast of America. Then he crossed the Pacific Ocean to finish up in Tientsin.

He became a travelling tuner for Robinson's Piano Company in Victoria Road and was often sent to work in a province west of Peking, deep in the Interior, where he tuned the pianos of missionaries and war-lords. These pianos were the relics of a huge consignment which had been sent to China from London in the late 1800s. Someone in London had calculated that as China was now open to Western ways, out of the 200 million women there, at least one in every 200 would surely wish to learn to play the piano. As a result of that logic, thousands of unwanted pianos rotted in the godowns of Hong Kong and Shanghai.

Mad Mac knew a lot about the early history of the British in China. One day I showed him the small clay figure that Y Jieh had bought for me in the market-place. 'That's General Gordon!' he said right away. He told me how, after the British and French had captured Tientsin, General Gordon had fought for the Emperor of China against the Tai Ping rebels near Shanghai, and had been awarded the Imperial Order of the Peacock Feather and the Yellow Waistcoat, China's highest military honours.

Pat and I needed no telling why Mad Mac had been given his nickname. He was unlike any foreigner we knew. He could speak three Chinese dialects and could also read and write Chinese characters. He lived alone and would disappear for weeks on end in the Interior. When in company, he often upset people with his remarks. Once he said something about Irish soldiers in the British Army which infuriated Captain O'Riordan, whose former regiment, the Connaught Rangers, had mutinied in India.

If he was in Tientsin, Mad Mac always spent New Year's Day with us. Like the Chinese, he felt there was something religious about the start of a new year.

At dinner we had the bustard which the Chinese owner of the butcher's shop in the market sent us for a present. He also sent us a red card. On it was the Chinese character *Fu* . . . Happiness. *Fu* was the character on the Boxers' red head scarves and I used to wonder if the butcher was a member of their secret society.

The bustard's dark flesh had a bitter taste. Only Mad Mac really liked eating it. Bustards came from the fringe of the Gobi desert west of Peking, he said as he helped himself to more. Staring at my plate, I saw our lean and tough old bustard stalking among wild camels on a yellow plateau and then running desperately before it was brought down by a hunter's gun. I heard Mad Mac laughing and my plate swam back into focus. Try as I might, I couldn't enjoy eating the bird.

When my father returned home from a tour of duty, Mad Mac would be sure to appear. He enjoyed hearing my father singing ballads about County Clare and he would join in the choruses. His Highland accent sounded very like my father's Irish brogue, but Pat could tell the difference. Upstairs in our bedroom, Pat would make me laugh by imitating Mad Mac. 'Aye, just a wee nip,' Pat would say, sounding just like him.

Pat was also good at imitating Brother Faust of the Marist Brothers. He had a fiery red nose and small shrewd eyes. His white hair, moustache and ragged beard always looked untidy and his shiny black soutane was stained with grease. He had the tantalizing habit of letting the ash on the end of his cigarette grow longer and longer until at last it fell on his soutane.

It was Brother Faust who had given us the picture of St Patrick which hung in the place of honour over the fireplace in the drawing-room. In the picture St Patrick stood by a rocky sea shore. Behind him, in the distance, was an old Celtic round tower. Shamrock sprouted from a rock beside him. He had a handsome face with a well-trimmed brown beard. He wore a golden mitre and a green chasuble which reached down to his knees. Under the chasuble, an alb, a long white garment with neatly folded pleats, fell to his red slippers. In one hand he held a shepherd's crook with a brass top. His other hand pointed at some snakes which were crawling away from him as fast as they could towards the sea. Brother Faust told us that snakes were the lowest things in all creation and that ever since St Patrick had driven them away, Ireland was the only place in the world where there were no snakes.

When Brother Faust, Mad Mac and my father were together in the drawing-room, they drank glasses of velvety-looking black stout and sometimes whiskey as well.

Brother Faust's favourite subject was Ireland and he did most of the talking. But when Captain and Mrs O'Riordan visited us, the Captain took charge of the conversation. Like Brother Faust, he was a native of Dublin, but he came from a more fashionable quarter, Blackrock.

After serving in India, the Captain had retired from the army and found employment as a civilian quartermaster at the British barracks in Tientsin, where his duties included buying food and coal for the garrison. Recently he had been appointed to serve on the Watch Committee, a post of which he was very proud.

Mrs O'Riordan was a nervous little woman. She was full of

advice for my mother, who called her 'a true friend in need'.

'The Captain thinks you should grow your own vegetables and keep chickens in your backyard,' Mrs O'Riordan said to my mother one evening. 'The war-lord Wu Pei Fu is marching towards Tientsin and might easily besiege us. And there's the Lotus. They say that hundreds of them are living in disguise in the Concession.' She stopped and blushed when she noticed that the Captain, who was about to make a pronouncement, was eyeing her.

He stood in front of the fireplace with his hands behind his back. A heavy man, he had a trim little moustache and bushy eyebrows which almost hid his eyes. The trousers of his grey tweed suit were neatly creased and his brown shoes were highly polished. 'In my opinion,' said the Captain, glancing round at everyone in the room to make sure they were listening, 'no one can see into the heart or mind of a Chinaman. He is inscrutable. Absolutely inscrutable.' He repeated the word with relish. Mrs O'Riordan's large doe-like eyes gazed at her husband with devotion.

'I'm bound to agree with you,' said Brother Faust, tugging at his rough little beard with one hand while the other held a lighted cigarette. 'But what about the Irish? It's hard to read some of our minds too, is it not? Come to think of it, they've a lot in common, the Irish and the Chinese. They both have long memories for a start.'

'Too long. Much too long,' said the Captain, shaking his head. 'It's the curse of Ireland, all that talk of the old heroes. And much of it invented too!' He rounded on Brother Faust and his cheeks flushed. 'If you'll forgive me saying so, Brother, and you Stephen, many of the brave things said about the Fenian rebels and the Easter Rising of 1916 were imagined by Irish exiles in America. It's easy to be a rebel at a distance and to prattle on about the "plough and the stars" when you're sitting in a bar in the middle of New York.'

'All the same, it was terrible the way they executed the leaders of the Rising,' replied Brother Faust, 'shooting a handful of them day after day for a week, and deaf to all pleas for mercy. The only one the British reprieved was de Valera. And do you know why, Captain? Because he was born in America and the President stepped in to save him.'

Mad Mac, who had been sipping his drink quietly in a corner, lifted his head and said, 'The Irish and the Chinese may have things in common, but do any of you know about the time the Irish persecuted the Chinese in California?' Everyone turned to look at him. 'Persecution?' said the Captain. 'That's a strong word, sir.'

'Aye, persecution,' said Mad Mac. 'It was when the Chinese coolies were building the Central Pacific railway line. Gangs of Irishmen set their fierce dogs on them and robbed and beat them in order to scare them away. In San Francisco, too, the Irish stoned poor Chinese laundry workers. All because the Chinese worked hard for very little money.'

There was silence for a few seconds. Even the Captain was at a loss for words. Then my father got up and filled everyone's glass. 'It's time you were in bed,' my mother said to Pat and me.

'How about a song, Stephen?' Brother Faust asked.

'Yes, capital idea,' said the Captain, 'give us "The Old Bog Road".' Mrs O'Riordan clapped her hands with excitement. 'Oh do, Stephen,' she said, 'it's my favourite.'

'Come on you young hooligans, off to bed with you,' the Captain said, wagging his finger at me.

On my way up the stairs, I heard the opening words of my father's old song:

> 'Sure t'was gathering time on the old bog road
> By Raftery's half-way house. . . .'

For a change, Pat was in no mood for mimicry. In bed we talked about the Irish in California. Our Uncle Joe lived there. He was a member of the Fenian Brotherhood, who were anti-British and raised funds to support the rebels in Ireland. Sometimes letters came from Uncle Joe urging my father to join the Fenians, but he was too easy-going to trouble about taking sides, let alone to bother to answer a letter.

'You don't think Uncle Joe stoned any Chinese, do you?' I asked Pat. He did not say anything and I realized he was fast asleep.

Downstairs someone opened the drawing-room door and the voices of Mad Mac and my father drifted up to me:

'T'is scattering time on the old bog road
By Raftery's half-way house.
I'm riding along and singing a song,
Though weary the day has been,
For I know I'll find a heart that's kind
At the end of the old boreen.'

IV

'When blossom falls from the cherry tree, .
Orioles come to the Northern Plain.'

Many times in our backyard I heard Jieh-jieh sing this song
about the golden orioles that passed through Tientsin in the
spring on their way northwards to Manchuria. They did not
stay long. The brief resting place of these elusive black-and-
yellow birds was the Russian Park, the only place in Tientsin
where there was a wood. Y Jieh called it the Garden of the
Orioles.

As a special treat, Y Jieh would take me there in the ferry
which crossed the Sea River. We never went in winter when the
river was frozen, although Pat used to go over with two of his
Siberian friends in a sledge called a *pai-ze* which the ferryman
propelled with a long spiked pole.

Even after the thaw it was often too difficult for the ferry to
cross. Sometimes the river was in full spate and the current was
too strong. At other times, after a drought, it was reduced to a
muddy trickle and smelt worse than the creek. There was
usually a dredger working in the middle of the channel. As its
buckets trundled one after the other into the water and then,
with a groaning noise, came up again laden with mud, it looked
like a many-headed monster fighting a losing battle to clear a
way to the sea.

The busiest ships on the river were the flat-bottomed
sampans. They queued up to escape from the maze of narrow
creeks into the river, where they carried all sorts of cargo along
the river front.

Two or three steamers and the gunboat HMS *Hollyhock* were

nearly always berthed near the Customs House on the British bund. When there was a grave emergency, HMS *Hollyhock* would be joined by her sister ship HMS *Foxglove*.

Up river from the Customs House, stretching as far as the French section called the Quai de France, was a row of small godowns. Lines of coolies, each carrying a sack on his back, moved incessantly between the ships and the godowns.

About a hundred yards down river from the Customs House was a small pier. This was the mooring place of the ferry, a wide raft which took us across to the Russian side of the river. If we had to wait for the ferry, I would lean against the wooden handrail at the end of the pier and look down at the swirling water. I liked to imagine the emperor's junks, in days gone by, sailing up this muddy river with precious cargoes for the Forbidden Palace, while pirates on board their sampans lurked in the creeks, waiting for prey.

Underneath the pier, in the side of the river bank just above the water line, were ten heavy wooden doors secured with iron bars. Behind these doors, which looked as if they had not been opened for centuries, were the ancient underground caves which had been store places during the Ming dynasty. Whenever I looked at the old doors, I used to imagine that gruesome things were hidden behind them. A skeleton, maybe, of some wretch who had been imprisoned by a wicked mandarin.

Across the river, you could see the trees of the Russian Park and, beside them, the onion-shaped dome of the Russian Orthodox church. This little church served Russians of many kinds. In Romanoff Avenue, which led from the river bank up to the church, lived the early settlers and their descendants who had established the Russian Concession here before 1900. They had many friends among the French and the British.

Then, in 1904, a wave of destitute Russians had arrived from Manchuria after their humiliating defeat by the Japanese. Most of them were the families of soldiers and sailors. Driven to begging and prostitution, they found some relief in drunkenness. They were an embarrassment to the settlers and lived apart in the long and bleak Caucasus Road in the northern outskirts of the Concession.

Following the Russian revolution in 1917, some Tsarist exiles, or White Russians as they were called, made their way overland to Tientsin. Those who could afford it went on to America. The poorer White Russians deigned to share Romanoff Avenue with the early settlers. Last of all came the dark-skinned, rough-tongued Siberians.

The best visit I ever made to the Russian Park was with Y Jieh and Jieh-jieh early one May. The long raft was packed with Chinese and there were also a few Russians near us who smelt of sour gaoliang wine. The ferryman rowed standing by his big stern oar. First we battled against the tide for a long way, then we floated in with it to the far shore.

After landing, we walked past the old houses in Romanoff Avenue until we came to the church with its strange dome and cross. Outside it was a row of cannons which the Russian Army had used during the Boxer Rising. A Russian wearing a smock and a soldier's cap on the back of his head was cutting the grass between two of the cannons. He worked very slowly with a sickle. When he noticed us he stood upright and stared at us as if he was a little drunk or a little mad. At the park gate I looked back over my shoulder. He was still standing there staring after us.

Unlike Victoria Park with its neat flower-beds and paths, this park was a stretch of wild woodland where long grass and trees of several kinds grew. You could run barefoot, play hide-and-seek, and walk down to the pond at the far edge of the wood for a picnic. If you looked between the trees there, you could see, far away towards the northern horizon, what appeared to be a long barricade; it was the beginning of the gaoliang fields.

On our way to the pond that day, we came to a small glade. We were about to cross it when we heard a bird singing. We stood still. Above us the branches were full of birds. They made splashes of yellow as they flew from tree to tree. Golden orioles! We sank down into the long grass. It was a magical moment. How lucky we are, I thought. By tomorrow these birds might be off to their northern forests, lost to the human eye. 'Sing us the song of the golden orioles, Jieh-jieh,' I asked her.

'When blossom falls from the cherry tree,
Orioles come to the Northern Plain.'

Her voice sounded so happy. What a different person Jieh-jieh seemed here in this small wood. She was like a flower that had opened in the sun.

Later that afternoon, we were leaving the park for the ferry when, from the direction of the river, we heard a whirring noise and strange, unearthly cries. 'The wild geese,' exclaimed Y Jieh. I looked up. Flying in an arrow formation, twelve or more large grey birds winged over us. In a moment they had disappeared beyond the trees, but Y Jieh remained for a long time looking up into the sky. Disturbed by her strange mood, I grasped her hand and tugged her. At last she looked down again. 'You seemed so different just now, Y Jieh,' I said. 'As if you could see further than the end of the world.'

'This is the time the wild geese fly away from the marshlands to Shanhaikwan,' she said. 'They always turn north over this wood.'

Many times after that we saw the wild geese fly away in the spring; sometimes they were followed by flights of cranes on their way to Manchuria.

At supper in the backyard that night, I told Sung Ge-ge all about our picnic and how happy Jieh-jieh had been in the wood. He laughed and sang in his hoarse voice:

'The caged bird longs for the old wood,
The fish in the net thinks of its native pool.'

Jieh-jieh pushed him and told him to stop. 'Never mind, Jieh-jieh,' I said, 'if you were a caged bird I would set you free.' She looked at me without saying anything. Then she smiled and put a hand on my shoulder. She smelt of garlic and white lotus blossom.

□

When Pat was eight years old and I was six, we went to a junior school in Gordon Road, run by the British Municipal Council. My mother was anxious that our English should be improved. All Pat's friends were Siberians, and I was nearly always downstairs with the servants, speaking Chinese.

Captain O'Riordan said that learning to speak good English was a most important part of a boy's education. It was a pity, he went on, that neither Stephen Power nor Mad Mac had been schooled at all. They set us a bad example. It was not their fault, of course, for they had little chance in wild country places like West Clare. At this my mother blushed furiously. It was a shameful family secret and a constant embarrassment to her that my father's mother had only Irish and not a word of English, and that the few letters which came from the Powers in Ireland were written by the village scribe.

Being Catholics, we should really have been sent to St Louis College run by the Marist Brothers, but Captain O'Riordan had advised against it. With all respect to Brother Faust, he said, St Louis was full of Russians and half-castes taught by French Brothers. What little English we had was certain to deteriorate there.

Most of the pupils at the Gordon Road school were British and American. They wore much smarter clothes than Pat and me. Everything in my classroom was neat and tidy, including Miss Evans, our teacher, who always wore a white starched collar. I sat behind a girl named Helen Gable, the daughter of an American army officer. She had long golden hair down to her shoulders and smelt of Palmolive soap.

To improve our English, Miss Evans read us passages from Charles Dickens. They were mostly tales of woe about poor people in London. One day when she was reading *Great Expectations*, my mind wandered and I gazed out of the window. General Gordon must have walked along this road when he was planning and mapping the British Concession, I thought. Little did he know then that one day he would be given the Peacock Feather and the Yellow Waistcoat by the Emperor of China. . . . After a while I realized that Miss Evans had stopped reading. Everyone in the room was staring at me.

'What were you thinking about, Brian?' Miss Evans asked.
'General Gordon.'
The other children laughed and Miss Evans looked angry.
'Say "Miss" when you answer.'
'Miss General Gordon,' I said, feeling confused.
There was more laughter and Miss Evans' neck reddened in a frightening way like a turkey I had once seen in the market-place. 'You must learn to stop day-dreaming,' she said.
We did not stay long at the British school. Pat began playing

truant. On the way to school he would leave me, saying that he would catch me up, then he would go off fishing in the Hidden Creek or cross over to the Russian Concession with his friends. At last the headmaster wrote a letter to my mother complaining that Pat was a bad influence.

Brother Faust came to my mother's rescue. He waved his cigarette about and stroked his beard as he spoke. 'The duty of a good Catholic parent . . . the bishop thinks . . . a sound religious education. . . .' So we were taken away from the British school after only one term there, and were told that we would be going to the Marist Brothers.

It was just before we went to our new school in the French Concession that the White Lotus society struck again. This time their prize was a fleet of six barges filled with grain which were sailing on the Grand Canal from Hankow to Tientsin. They were last seen about a mile from the terminus. Although a search was made in the network of creeks leading off the canal, no trace of the barges or their cargo was found.

Suspecting that there was an informer in the customs service, the Watch Committee ordered the interrogation of all customs officers in Hankow and Tientsin. My mother was very worried because my father was on duty in Hankow. I tried to talk to Pat about the raid and my father, but he treated it all as a joke.

At the door of our drawing-room one evening, I heard Brother Faust reassuring my mother. 'The fact that Stephen is in Hankow won't tell against him. After all, there were two other officers there. It's just a routine inquiry, Grace. Ah, Brian,' he said, quickly changing the subject when he saw me walk into the room. 'Are you all ready for St Louis? We are looking forward to having you.'

□

The Emperor Napoleon I sat on a white charger and pointed his arm at a range of snow-capped mountains. He looked young and handsome and his eyes glittered with the fire of adventure. A little further along the corridor, an older-looking French officer stood on a muddy plain and pointed his sword at hundreds of Chinese who were defending a fort.

'Ah! You are studying our pictures already.' I turned round

and looked up at a tall thin man in a black soutane. From his neck there hung a pair of white tabs and below them, in the middle of his chest, a brass crucifix. It was Brother Superior.

A week before, my mother had brought us to this red-brick building in rue St Louis just inside the French Concession. We had all gone up to Brother Superior's room on the first floor. Three big windows looked out over a playground. Brother Superior sat at a desk in front of the middle window. I could hardly see his face against the sunlight. Brother Faust was there too. He gave me a wink which made me feel worse and I wished I was back at home in our backyard with Y Jieh and Sung Ge-ge.

'It is settled then, Madame,' said Brother Superior. 'Patrick here will go to Brother Alphonse's class. Brother Paul's class will be best for Brian. I understand he needs help with his English and French. . . . Yes, Brother Faust has explained to me. . . . Of course we will have to wean him from thinking and speaking only in Chinese.'

'My husband is away so much and I . . .'

'Yes, yes, Madame, I quite understand.'

Brother Superior stood up. He put his right hand deep in the large side pocket of his soutane and began to jingle a bunch of keys. It was his signal that the interview was over.

Now, standing in the entrance corridor, I could see his face clearly for the first time. His mouth smiled at you, revealing his teeth, but his eyes remained cold.

'I am glad to see you are interested in pictures,' he said. 'The Chinese say, do they not, that a picture is worth a thousand words.' He put on his spectacles and peered over my head at the picture of Napoleon. 'The conquest of Italy,' he said. 'Those are the Alps.' Then he led me to the other picture. 'General de Montauban, Count of Palikao, leading the attack against the Taku forts. After that he captured Tientsin . . . with the help of the British, of course. His third battle in China was at Palikao, between here and Peking. You will learn more about him in your history lessons – how, for instance, he was destined to serve the Emperor Napoleon III as his Prime Minister.' Brother Superior put his hand in his pocket and began to jingle his keys. 'But now I must take you to Brother Paul's classroom. He is waiting to welcome you on your first day with us.'

We walked along the ground-floor corridor until we came to a

door which Brother Superior opened. He beckoned me to follow
him in. There was a lot of scraping and clattering as the boys
stood up. Brother Paul was standing on a platform behind his
desk, pointing his cane at a large map of the world. At first he
looked flustered and a little annoyed at being interrupted, then
he lowered his cane and gave Brother Superior a thin, meek
smile.

Brother Superior walked onto the platform. 'Sit down, sit
down,' he said, waving his hands up and down. The boys
slumped down. There were about forty of them, sitting four to a
bench at long desks. 'Come here, Brian.' I stumbled up onto the
platform. Brother Superior took hold of my elbow. 'I am glad to
introduce your new colleague, Brian. You are already, shall I
say, an international class. Now you have a boy from Ireland,
the country of saints and scholars.' He smiled at his own words.
The boys all looked glum. I blushed and wished he would let go
of my elbow. I felt that Brother Paul was staring at me, but I did
not dare to look at him. 'Good, I will leave you with Brother
Paul.' At last Brother Superior let go of me and strode towards
the door. The boys half rose from their benches and quickly sat
down again.

Brother Paul came towards me. He had closely cropped fair
hair and pale blue eyes which were pink and watery and half
hidden behind small steel-rimmed glasses. He nearly always
stood in the shade, and the blinds in our classroom were kept
drawn if it was sunny outside. He rubbed his hands together
nervously. 'This is your place,' he said, showing me to a bench at
the far end of the front row by a window. The other three boys
moved up and I sat on the very edge of the bench, looking
straight ahead of me and trying to stop blushing.

'The Sahara is one of France's biggest territories. . . .' I only
half listened to Brother Paul and found refuge in the map of the
world. The French Empire was coloured bright green. One of
the biggest bright green places was French Indo-China in the
east. Above it, China was coloured yellow. To the north-east
was the Yellow Sea, Taku and, a little way up the Sea River,
Tientsin. On the other side of the map, the British Isles were a
dull pink colour. There, on the western edge of the world, as far
from Tientsin as possible, was the River Shannon and County
Clare where my father had promised to take me one day.

Half the boys in my class were boarders. Their dormitories were on the second floor, above the chapel and the Brothers' rooms. The rest, like myself, were day-boys. There were Russians from Manchuria, Siberians, French, Belgians, and a sprinkling of Turks, Armenians, Portuguese, Filipinos and Italians. We also had six or seven half-castes. Two of them sat on the same bench as me. Carlo Simoes, a sad-looking boy, had a Portuguese father and a Chinese mother. Bobby Thomas had a Korean mother. His father, a Welsh seaman, worked on a passenger ship. Both Carlo and Bobby were boarders. A half-caste was the worst thing you could be, and I used to feel sorry for them.

Fifteen of us were Catholics, the rest were Russian Orthodox, Jewish, Muslim or nothing. At the beginning of each day we all stood up in our classroom and said a Hail Mary for the conversion of the boys who were not Catholics. . . . 'Mother of God pray for us sinners now and at the hour of our death, amen.' It always moved me to hear Yura Shirokoff, my Manchurian-Russian neighbour, humbly reciting the Hail Mary for his own conversion. But the Siberians, Kabuliansky, Gurevich and Baranoff, who were in the row behind us, always remained silent.

Behind Brother Paul, on either side of the map of the world, were two large coloured pictures made of oil paper. One was of heaven, the other of hell. Purgatory and limbo were at the back of the room. In hell Lucifer and his devils, carrying long black forks, drove people down into the red and orange flames. It was frightening to look at, but fascinating. Most of the damned were naked women. One plump woman, wearing nothing but a necklace of pearls, reminded me a little of Grandmother d'Arc. If I spent too long staring at this picture, I would look up to find Brother Paul's watery eyes on me. I would turn quickly to look at the picture of heaven.

At the top of heaven, the Holy Trinity sat on white clouds, surrounded by angels and saints with haloes. They were receiving a long queue of good people who climbed up towards them. First came popes in tiaras and cardinals in red hats, followed by bishops and priests in golden vestments. Then came religious brothers in black soutanes and white neck bands. At the bottom of the picture were the ordinary people. They were

led by a family holding each other's hands as they stood
patiently in the queue, their eyes shining with devotion. The
children looked up at their mother, she looked up at her
husband, and he looked up towards the Holy Trinity.

The father of this upright family was dressed in a dark suit and
stiff white collar and tie. He looked just like Monsieur Ledoux,
the director of the Banque de l'Indo Chine, who had the front
pew in Notre Dame.

Whenever I looked at this family in heaven, I couldn't help
comparing it with my own family. The only time we had all
been out together was one St Patrick's Day when we had gone
with our parents to mass at Notre Dame. Pat and I wore our new
sailor suits which Uncle Jim, who was in the Royal Navy, had
sent us. Each of us had a sprig of shamrock and my father had
also put a sprig on top of the picture of St Patrick in our drawing-
room. The shamrock had come in a box from our Uncle Joe in
America. It wasn't real shamrock, my father said, for that could
only grow in Ireland, but it was the next best thing.

At the church door, my father left us and went off to talk to
some of his Irish friends from the Customs who were in the
courtyard. During mass he didn't come to our pew, but stood at
the back of the church with his friends. My mother kept her face
buried in her hands and I could sense that she was upset. Was
she still thinking about what had happened in our drawing-
room the night before? Brother Faust had put down his glass of
frothy black stout and the yellow tobacco-stained fingers of his
hand had trembled as he stroked his beard. 'Let's face it, Steve,'
he said. 'The customs service has always run the opium traffic in
China.' My mother blushed down to her neck and told Pat and
me to leave the room. At the door I heard Brother Faust say, 'No
offence intended, Steve,'

We all stood up for the last gospel. Glancing round, I saw that
my father and his friends had gone. After mass Pat ran off to the
bund and I went home with my mother in a rickshaw. It was
miserable in the rickshaw and I wished I had been quick enough
to escape with Pat.

□

A bell clanged at 10.30 in the morning for recreation time, and we all rushed out on to the playground of earth and stones. A Brother threw a football into the air and the whole school of about a hundred and fifty boys, big and small, chased after it for fifteen minutes. There were no goal-posts; the aim was to dribble the ball for as long as you could. We did it again in mid-afternoon. This hectic chase, which was obligatory, went on whatever the weather was like: in hot sunshine, in rain, or in winter when the ground was covered with freezing snow. You had to be fast and strong to reach the ball and keep it at your feet for long. Gurevich and Kabuliansky from my class sometimes got the ball, but in all my time at St Louis I never once managed even to touch it. Any boy who gave up the chase was sure to be spotted. Once I was about to steal away to a quiet corner when I glanced up and saw Brother Superior standing at his window, looking down at me.

St Louis always beat the British school at football and athletics, although the British school had more boys to choose from, two army coaches on the staff, a gymnasium and fine playing-fields. People said it was the tough Siberians at St Louis who made all the difference, boys like Ibragimoff and Kravchuk, but the wild chase around the playground, twice a day, must have had something to do with it.

The rivalry between the two schools went deeper than sports. The British school's teachers, who were called masters and mistresses, had university degrees and were Protestants. Some of them were missionaries. Their pupils were mostly British and American, but there were also a few White Russians. It was reputed to be one of the best schools in China. Good as it might have been, the wealthier British parents sent their children to boarding schools in England.

Although St Louis was a French school, our lessons were in English because it was the main language of commerce among foreigners in Tientsin. But the English we spoke was not the English of the British school. Ours was spoken in a strong Siberian-Russian accent and laced with strangely coined slang. Even Brother Paul's French began to sound more and more Siberian. We suffered for our hybrid tongue, for we were the butt of endless jokes by the British school boys. In return, St Louis boys were always scoffing at the British school with its mixed classes of smartly dressed boys and girls and its White

Russian pupils who put on airs. Once Captain O'Riordan spoke
sharply to Pat and me. 'You may jeer at the British school over
football and running,' he said, 'but when it comes to passing
exams, they have you beaten easily. As for that so-called English
you're speaking, Pat,' he added, 'you sound more like a Siberian
bandit every day.'

The Siberian bandits at St Louis invented a game called
'beedka' which they were allowed to play after school hours. It
was played with cigarette cards, which most boys collected and
which were a form of currency at school. The cards varied in
value. Pictures of famous battles were worth more than the
animals and insects series. The ones with the least value were the
Japanese and Chinese cards with their pictures of landscapes
and scenes from ancient stories. At the start of the game, each
player had to put a cigarette card of the right value on the
ground. A circle, about two feet in diameter, was then drawn
round the cards. From a mark, ten yards from the cards, each
player in turn threw an old rubber shoe-heel at them. If you
knocked a card out of the circle, it became yours. A really good
throw would clear the whole pack of cards out of the circle and
earn you a small fortune. The leading players were Kravchuk
and Nakvasin. Pat, who was a friend of theirs, became very good
at beedka. He played it a lot during the midday break and often
didn't come home for anything to eat.

At twelve o'clock the bell rang for the end of the morning's
classes and the day-boys usually walked home for the hour and a
half's break. The boarders crowded round a bearded old
Siberian at the school gate who sold *piroshkees*, a Siberian
dumpling filled with oily cabbage and onion. The old man had
no shoes and his feet were bound in newspaper and rags. When
we had any coppers, some of us day-boys would join in the rush
for *piroshkees*. One day I couldn't get through the crowd to the
old man before they were all sold out. Yura Shirokoff, who sat
next to me in class, broke his in two and gave me half.

Yura and I became friends. He came from northern
Manchuria. His father had been killed fighting against the
Bolsheviks in Siberia. His mother, who had brought him to
Tientsin two years before, worked for a dressmaker in the old
German Concession. She worked long hours and at weekends as
well in order to send him to St Louis where he was a boarder. I

helped Yura as best I could with his English and in exchange he answered a constant stream of questions from me about Manchuria.

Manchuria! Land of the tiger! How often I had taken our battered old atlas downstairs to talk to Sung Ge-ge about that wild country of steppe land and mountains where there lived not only Chinese, but also Russians, Cossacks, Siberians and Koreans. Now I had a friend who could show me on the big classroom map places like Mukden, which was so often raided by bandits, ancient Chang Chun, Town of Eternal Spring, and Harbin, the Trans-Siberian Railway town where he had been born.

Six thousand miles east of Moscow, Harbin was the last stop before the long journey from Europe ended at the port of Vladivostok. From Harbin a branch line ran southwards down the central plain of Manchuria, through the gateway in the Great Wall at Shanhaikwan and on to Tientsin.

Down that line, Yura told me, the Allies had retreated in 1919 at the end of their disastrous expedition. Their commander-in-chief was Kolchak, an old Tsarist admiral who was President of the Far Eastern Republic of Siberia. Before they quit Siberia the Allies did a terrible thing. Harried by the rapidly advancing Bolsheviks and anxious to make good their escape, they surrendered Kolchak to the Bolsheviks, who shot him. . . . My thoughts wandered to Wang the park policeman. So that was his guilty secret! Now I knew why he looked so worried whenever the veteran Russian officer came to Victoria Park.

Yura said that in the railway towns along the Manchurian plain where the ogre Semenov and his Cossacks rode, there still lived groups of Siberian exiles who had not managed to find their way abroad or even to come down to Tientsin.

□

Brother Paul gave us religious instruction. He knew a lot about hell and the Devil. One of his best stories was about the Devil and the Freemasons.

In a small wood-panelled room, chairs were drawn up to a table. A Freemasons' meeting was about to take place. A brave Marist Brother stole into the empty room to find out their secrets. Hearing footsteps coming, he hid himself in a cupboard and kept its door slightly ajar. The Freemasons came in and sat at the table. They were all dressed in smart business suits. Suddenly there was a puff of smoke and the Devil appeared at the head of the table. You could tell he was the Devil because, although he was dressed like the others, he had a cloven hoof.

The Freemasons bowed to the Devil, but he was very disturbed and angry. He looked around, sniffed, and said, 'There is a Catholic in this room!' In the uproar which followed, the Devil rushed around the room, searching. He looked under the table and then he came to the cupboard and flung open its door to reveal not only a Catholic, but a Marist Brother! There was further uproar as the Freemasons came running up. The Marist Brother was trapped and in great danger, but he kept calm, took hold of his crucifix and held it up. The Devil staggered back, covered his face with his hands and, howling with pain, fled from the room followed by all the Freemasons.

Brother Paul's eyes were shining as he came to the end of the story.

'Yes, Brian?' he asked when I put up my hand.

'Was it you, Brother, who hid in the cupboard?'

'No. It happened to one of our Brothers in France. Now remember, if you carry a crucifix wherever you go, you need not be afraid of the Devil.'

Many of the leading British businessmen in Tientsin were Freemasons. Their Master was Mr Peebles, the chairman of the British Municipal Council. The senior Freemasons were called Worshipful Brothers, but Brother Paul said they had no right to that title. Their meeting place, the Masonic Temple, was next to d'Arc's Hotel. Whenever I passed it, I would think of Brother Paul's story of the Devil, and I would wonder what secret things were going on inside.

Although he often talked to us about hell, heaven and purgatory, Brother Paul said very little about limbo. It was the place where good people who were not baptized Christians went after they died. Many of them were babies. Although they did not burn in flames like the wicked in hell, they could not be really happy because they would never see God.

The picture of limbo at the back of our classroom had quiet colours and none of the red, black and orange of the other pictures. Small children and men and women from Africa, India and China, looking calm and wistful, wandered through a woodland glade. In the distance, above the green trees, you could see pale blue mountains.

□

'*Introibo ad altare Dei*,' recited Brother Paul.
'*Ad Deum qui laetificat juventutem meam*,' we mumbled in response.
'I will go unto the altar of God.'
'Unto God who giveth joy to my youth.'
We were practising serving mass in the school chapel. In our servers' manuals the English and Latin words were side by side. It was quite easy to say the Latin even though I didn't fully understand it; it sounded so much like Chinese. But the prayerbook English was very strange and stilted.

When we forgot what to do at the altar, Brother Paul signalled to us with his hands. Now genuflect, now move the big book from one side of the altar to the other, now ring the bell, now offer wine and water to the priest, now put out the candles, now genuflect.

Brother Paul said that the proper word for an altar boy was 'acolyte'. It was a privilege to be one. Acolytes were not shown in the picture of heaven in our classroom, but they came after the priests and brothers and before the ordinary people.

The feast of St Louis, King of France, was a school holiday. All the acolytes attended mass in their red cassocks and white surplices. I was wearing mine for the first time and felt very self-conscious as we walked in pairs from the sacristy into the crowded chapel. We sat in the front pew, across the aisle from the Brothers. My mother sat with the other parents behind us. She felt proud because Pat was one of the two boys chosen to serve mass that day.

'*Dico autem vobis, quia omnia habenti dabitur. . . .*' 'But I say unto you that to everyone that hath shall be given, and he shall abound; and from him that hath not, even that which he hath shall be taken from him.' The priest finished reading the gospel. He turned to face us and began to preach. 'My dear brethren. St Louis, as you know, was not only a saint and a king, he also led two glorious crusades to try to recapture the Holy Land. During the second of his crusades, he was struck down by the plague and carried to Tunis where he died.' The priest paused and looked at us. 'We too, like St Louis, patron saint of this school, must become crusaders and lead lives of service for the Faith. Some of you acolytes may, if God wills it, become Marist Brothers yourselves one day. . . .' Without having to turn round and look at her, I could sense that my mother's face was glowing and her heart leaping at the possibility that Pat might one day become a Marist Brother. Her worries about him would then be over.

After mass Brother Paul led all the acolytes outside to the playground where our photograph was taken. Luckily, being a holiday, there was no one about, otherwise Kravchuk, Nakvasin and some of the other Siberian beedka players would have feasted their eyes on our starched and pleated white surplices, our red cassocks and the sight of Brother Paul grinning and patting us on the back. After that dangerous exposure, Pat never again risked being seen by his friends in the trappings of an altar boy. When due to serve mass, he would turn up so late that he was marked down as unreliable. At last, Brother Paul despaired of him and struck him off the roll of servers. It seemed that we were not to have a Brother Patrick in our family after all.

□

Near our school, on the British side of rue St Louis, stood a high brick wall which hid a Chinese war-lord's palace. Above the wall you could see the tops of some trees. Branches of weeping ash and wistaria hung down the wall in splashes of yellow-green and purple. The big iron gate with spikes on top of it was always kept closed.

Yura Shirokoff thought that the war-lord kept wild animals in his garden and that there might even be a tiger there. I longed to look into the garden. It was just possible to climb the wall for there were one or two footholds where the brick was worn, but you were certain to be arrested if you were seen.

On my way home one day, when there were few people about, I plucked up courage and climbed to the top of the wall. I grabbed hold of a wistaria branch and lay there for a while, feeling frightened and dizzy. As I recovered my breath, I dared to look about me. Beyond some trees I could see a pavilion with a curved roof. Nothing stirred. Then a movement below me caught my eye. Looking down, I saw, through some branches, a big circular cage standing on a stone-paved floor. A huge bird glared at me through the bars. It was an eagle! I caught my breath in wonder. One of its legs was chained to an iron perch. The eagle's feathers had bald patches and it looked old, but its yellow eyes were fierce and defiant. A feeling of awe mixed with pity came over me, and then a strange sensation I had never known before; as I watched it, I felt that a bond existed between me and this eagle, and I heard myself whispering, 'I promise that I will come back and see you again.'

Dropping to the ground, I ran back to St Louis as fast as I could to tell Yura what I had seen. Two figures were standing by the school gate. One was Kravchuk. The other had his back to me, but there was no mistaking the fringe of carrot-coloured hair round the bald head, the walking-stick and the old brown shoes. Mad Mac! What was he doing there? And why was he talking to Kravchuk? Puzzled, I turned and walked away for I did not want Mad Mac to know that I had seen him.

V

From my seat by the window in Brother Paul's classroom, I could see the tops of some trees. They were beyond a row of houses at the back of the school. Sometimes when the trees swayed in the wind, I relived the day Y Jieh, Jieh-jieh and I had walked in the Russian Park.

> 'When blossom falls from the cherry tree
> Orioles come to the Northern Plain.'

Jieh-jieh's quiet voice mingled with the sighing of the wind in the trees. I ran through the wild long grass and came to the edge of a glade. . . . A silence in the classroom brought me back. Brother Paul was looking at me angrily. 'What are you dreaming about now?' he asked. 'You must learn to pay attention, Brian. Begin again, Igor.'

Igor Kabuliansky read: 'One day, when the Emperor Napoleon I was near the end of his life, one of his loyal staff asked him: "Sire, what has been the happiest day of your life?" With tears of joy in his eyes, the great emperor answered: "The day of my First Holy Communion."'

When you were seven years old, Brother Paul explained, you reached the age of reason. Then, if you were in a state of grace, you could receive Holy Communion. The happiest day of my life was approaching! Lately, I had been thinking a lot about receiving the body and blood of Christ. One of my solos was the old French communion hymn '*Mon Dieu je ne suis pas digne de vous recevoir*'. I had sung it in Notre Dame at Pat's First Holy Communion. The memory of that day brought a slight misgiving. Pat had not behaved as if it was a special day in his

76

life. After mass he had just gone fishing at the Hidden Creek. Perhaps, I hoped, communion had altered him in some way that I hadn't noticed.

At home in our backyard I sat beside Y Jieh and helped her to shell the peas before supper. In another corner Sung Ge-ge was playing 'The moon over Mount Tai' on his one-string violin. A bat, the first of the evening, fluttered over our heads and then came to rest in one of its hiding-places.

I tried to explain to Y Jieh about confession and the need for one's soul to be in a state of grace before communion, but it was very difficult. 'Anyway, Y Jieh,' I said, seeing that she was not impressed, 'you and Jieh-jieh won't have to burn in flames when you die, for you will both go to a place called limbo. That's where all good people go who do not follow the teaching of the Lord of Heaven. In that place you will be able to walk among beautiful trees like the wood in the Russian Park and there will be a river too, and maybe in the spring golden orioles will come and sing to you.'

Beyond the garden wall the flower pedlar shuffled past on his way to another street corner. I could just see his head and the bamboo pole resting on his thin shoulders. Tomorrow he would be back again. The whole yard was filled with peace.

□

'Father, this is my first confession.'

'Yes, my child.'

I could not see Father Molinari through the wooden grille in the confession box, but I could smell stale wine mixed with tobacco.

'Yes, my child?' he repeated.

I felt too ashamed to speak. Tomorrow in this church I would be making my First Communion. How could I tell him about my sin? When he heard it, would he refuse to give me communion? At last I blurted it out.

'Father, I have been wishing I could go to limbo when I die, instead of heaven.'

There was a long silence. Father Molinari sighed deeply.

'How many times, my child?'

'About seven times, I think.'

'You know, do you not, that the souls in limbo never see God?'
'Yes, Father.'
'You must pray to God for faith, my child. Remember the words in your catechism. He made you to know Him, love Him, and serve Him in this world and in the next. For your penance you will say ten times the Glory be to the Father. Now make a good act of contrition. *Absolvo te.* . . . Go in peace, my child.'

□

The First Communion procession moved slowly up the aisle of Notre Dame, boys on the right and girls, wearing veils, on the left. We were all dressed in white. Even the cover of my new prayer book was white.

At the altar rail the girls knelt down while the boys went on up the red carpeted steps to the sanctuary, which was forbidden to women. Each of us had his own prie-dieu. I knelt at mine and gazed at the altar with its arched marble columns soaring up to heaven like distant mountain tops. In a little while I would be receiving the body and blood of Christ for the first time. The thought filled me with awe.

When mass began I opened my new prayer book. It was called *The Garden of the Soul.* Inside the cover was a picture of the Last Supper. Christ was handing pieces of bread, which he had changed into his body, to the simple country people who were his disciples. Several of them were fishermen. They made me think of my father's people in West Clare in the days when they still had their curraghs. I wished that my father could have been here today, but he was away in Shanghai.

In the background of the picture of the Last Supper, behind Christ, were three large windows which opened out on to a garden with strange-looking trees in it, unlike any of the trees in the Russian Park. I was wondering whether they had golden orioles in Palestine, when the bell rang. '*Sanctus, sanctus, sanctus.* . . ,' Father Molinari recited, bowing before the wafer of bread. What a simple thing that wafer was, made from wheat grown by the peasants in some Chinese field.

'*Hoc est enim corpus meum.* . . . For this is my body.' Now Father Molinari was performing the miracle, the same miracle that Christ had performed at the Last Supper. That terrible power was given to all Catholic priests. It did not matter if they were bad-tempered and irritable like Father Molinari, no one could take that power from them.

'*Corpus Domini nostri Jesu Christi.* . . .' Father Molinari placed the small white wafer on the tip of my tongue and I swallowed it. I did not think or feel anything. Instead, a sensation of belief overwhelmed me. My soul was in command of me as it never would be again. This sensation of believing filled me with a happiness which no thought or feeling had ever done, and I remember hoping that it would never end.

After mass I walked in the procession down the aisle, only dimly aware of the faces of people in the congregation, for I was in that mysterious garden in the picture. Something warned me that there was sorrow hidden among its rocks and trees, but for the moment it was pure joy to be there in the garden of my soul.

Leaving the church, I crossed the courtyard where my mother was chatting to a group of proud parents. They did not notice me and I walked away quietly on my own, intent on my secret reverie of thanksgiving. '*Quid retribuam Dominum.* . . . What shall I give to the Lord in return for all that He has given to me?'

When I reached the Banque de l'Indo Chine at the corner of rue St Louis and Victoria Road, I saw a Chinese man and woman with a young girl about my age, sitting on the pavement. They were very thin and you could see their skin through the tears in their blue cotton rags. Their bare feet were caked in mud. It was easy to tell that they were peasants and had probably come off a sampan at the bund nearby. One or two Chinese were standing there looking at the peasants, and other people passing by began to walk over to see what was going on.

The woman stared at the ground while the girl sat beside her whimpering. The man looked about him wildly. At first I thought they were not well. But then the man grasped the girl by the wrist and cried out, '*Ni mai ma?* Will you buy? Will you buy?' With a shock I realized what was happening. The man and woman were selling their daughter. I had often heard about peasants selling their daughters when they had nothing to eat, but this was the first time I had ever seen them do it.

More people gathered and then a policeman by the Hong Kong and Shanghai Bank started to cross the road towards us. I walked away along Victoria Road towards the park, feeling sick and dizzy. In the park I sat on a bench and tried to think about the miracle of my First Communion, but I could see only the face of the woman staring at the ground while the girl whimpered.

That night, kneeling by my bed, I made another attempt to recapture that sensation of joy I felt after Father Molinari had given me the host. I opened my new white prayer book and tried to read the devotion called 'Aspirations after Communion'. But it was no good. I kept seeing the man selling his daughter on the street.

I had come to that hidden place of sorrow in the garden, and I knew that the wretched peasants were part of the everlasting agony of Christ.

□

A week after my First Communion, Pat saw a long line of peasants carrying bundles, walking by the canal district just outside the Concession. After that, there were daily reports of peasants being seen near Tientsin. Then, at last, we heard about the drought. For nearly two years there had been no rain in the region of the Yellow River estuary and thousands of peasants were migrating northwards towards Manchuria. Soldiers and police manned the boundaries to keep them out of Tientsin and on the move, but a few, like the family I had seen, infiltrated the Concessions. They slipped in at night on sampans along the canals and creeks. When day broke it was easy to spot the weak and exhausted, and they were soon rounded up. Only the strong escaped detection.

In the autumn the locusts came. Like the dust storms, they darkened the sky as they swarmed overhead before raining down on us. We all rushed to shut the doors and windows. My mother, who was terrified of them, became frantic. 'There you are,' she cried, her voice rising to a nervous shriek. 'I told you so. I knew they were coming. They always come after a drought.' Her piano lesson was stormy that evening. 'No, no, no!' she shouted at her pupil. 'B sharp, I said. Play that again.'

All night long the locusts flew with dull thuds against the window-panes. In the morning the garden was full of them. About two inches long and grey-brown in colour, they squirmed over each other in a vicious and silent tangle as they fought to get at the grass. Already our umbrella tree looked as naked as it did in the winter. More and more locusts, their wings whirring, dropped down from the sky. The poor Chinese collected piles of them from the gutters and took them home to cook and eat. Sung Ge-ge fried some and made a horrible smell in the kitchen. I tried one to be brave, and the nasty sour taste remained in my mouth for a long time.

In two days, the locusts devoured every flower and blade of grass in Victoria Park. Wang the park policeman enjoyed them. He sat on his bench eating them raw. It was horrifying to watch him. He pulled off their heads and wings and popped them into his mouth while they were still alive. He offered me one and roared with laughter when I ran away.

□

'Mad Mac is back!' I heard Pat call out, and rushed after him to the backyard. There he was, standing at the gate beside Pat who was now as tall as he was. You could tell Mad Mac had been on a long trip to the Interior. His fringe of hair, once so red, now looked like bits of rusty-coloured straw matting. The lines on his tanned face had been worn deeper by the wind and sand. His pale blue eyes had a yellow tinge as if the earth of the loess country was still reflected in them.

Mad Mac had been tuning pianos in mission houses scattered over a wide area of countryside. What a good spy he would make! I thought to myself. For, as well as the concert piano in Gordon Hall, he looked after the pianos in the British Officers' Mess, the headquarters of the Japanese High Command and in · the war-lord Feng Yu Hsiang's railway carriage.

He smiled when I told him with great excitement that next week Y Jieh was going to take me on my first visit to the canal district near the marshland. 'That's where she lived once,' he said. 'Well, it will be a good day's adventure for you. Tell me if you see any curlews. You should be just in time for them. They fly south in October.'

Early on a Saturday morning, I set off with Y Jieh, full of curiosity at what we were going to see. Was this the feeling that explorers had, I wondered, as we walked down Meadows Road and crossed a bridge over a creek. At last we came to the police hut which marked the south-eastern boundary of the British Concession. A Chinese policeman was sitting on a bench reading a newspaper. He nodded to us as we passed.

Soon after the hut, we left the road and its telegraph wires and climbed on to a dyke about six feet high, which had been built after the big flood in 1918. Before us, as far as we could see, was marshland; brown and yellow rushes and strips of water which glinted like silver in the early-morning sun. Above us, the huge blue sky looked wider than I had ever seen it.

'We're in the country! Hooray, the country!' I stretched out my arms and danced up and down. Y Jieh smiled. 'Where is your old home, Y Jieh?' She pointed to a line of small dusty willow trees. 'Over there, to the left.' As I proudly led the way along the top of the dyke, I heard a rustling noise at my feet and a green-and-yellow snake slid down the bank and disappeared among some rushes and muddy water. 'Quick, Y Jieh. A snake!' I cried. 'Don't be afraid,' she said, 'it won't hurt you.' But I felt nervous and let her go on ahead. Several times we turned left and right on the network of dykes and I completely lost my sense of direction.

When we were about two hundred yards from the willows, small clouds of tiny birds rose up and swirled over our heads. 'Rice birds,' Y Jieh said. Now and again a snipe would get up and fly rapidly away, weaving and keeping low. Then, as we were coming down from the dyke to a muddy path, I heard a plaintive cry coming from some rushes by a pool. 'Cour-lee, cour-lee.' I had never heard that cry before, and yet I felt I was remembering it from long ago. Suddenly I saw the birds. First one, then another two, then more. Six I counted altogether as they flew, twisting this way and that. They were brown coloured and had long thin curved beaks exactly as Mad Mac had described them. 'Curlews!' I whispered in wonder. Then they dropped down in another hidden place.

Y Jieh walked back to where I was standing lost in reverie. 'Did you see?'

'Yes, marsh birds,' she said. 'They'll fly away if you go after them.' We walked on along the path, but I kept turning round in case I should see the curlews. Once or twice I heard their haunting cry again and the sound made the country about us seem desolate. I felt cold and shivered.

At last we reached the willow trees. Behind them lay a canal about twenty yards wide. It was lined with small boats, all of which were packed with people. We walked along the canal bank under the trees. After we had passed five or six sampans and two old salt barges, we came to a small sampan half hidden among some reeds. It had a square prow and a stern that curved upwards. A roof of gaoliang stalks covered the hold in the stern.

A woman came out of the hold. She looked like Y Jieh, only she was younger. Behind her was a cluster of children, two boys and six girls. 'Welcome, welcome,' she said, helping us on board. She made me sit on a roll of bedding in the stern where an old fisherman was squatting by a charcoal brazier. Beside him were two iron pots, a grain basket and a broom.

The old man's name was Cheng. He grinned at me and said, 'You must eat something, you are tired.' We had cabbage, boiled gaoliang and tea. Nobody spoke much during the meal. The children, who were very shy, hid behind their mother and peered at me. The coarse yellow gaoliang grains tasted bitter and I had to make an effort to finish my bowlful. Maybe I would get used to it, I thought, if I lived in a boat on the canal. Mad Mac said that gaoliang was the one thing the poor in north China had. It was true when you thought about it. From gaoliang they got food, wine, thatching for their roofs, matting for their floors, baskets, brooms and many other things besides.

After a while, I turned to Cheng and said,' We saw a snake.' He laughed. 'There are many snakes here. Look!' he said, pointing over the side. A snake, with only its dark green head showing above the water, swam by in the middle of the canal, leaving an arrow of ripples behind it.

'Snakes are bad, aren't they?' I asked Cheng.

He laughed and slapped his thigh. 'No, they are good. You get medicine from them, and you can eat them.'

'But in my father's country, Ireland, they say snakes are bad, and a holy man, the hero of Ireland, drove all the snakes away into the sea.'

Cheng shook his head and said nothing.

'How far is the sea from here?' I asked him.

'He is always dreaming about the sea,' Y Jieh said.

Cheng laughed. 'I'll have to take him there one day. If you know the way through the canals and small creeks, you can reach the sea in about two days, but it is not easy to find the way.'

'You should take him to the watch-tower,' said the woman of the boat.

'Come,' said Cheng. We stepped on to the bank and walked to the end of the line of trees. The children followed us at a distance. Beyond the last tree was a mound of earth about twelve feet high, with steps cut in it. We climbed to the top. 'Look there,' said Cheng, pointing to the south. Square strips of dark brown swayed as they glided slowly across the flat land.

'What are they?' I asked.

'Those are the sails of the big junks on the Grand Canal. It is less than a mile from here.'

'Where is the sea?'

He pointed above the willow trees to the east. 'It is always misty here, but over there, beyond the reeds, are the mudflats of Taku. Beyond them is the sea.'

I turned round and looked back, westwards towards Tientsin. The roof of the British Country Club stood out clearly. Next to it was the racecourse. The hundreds of people who went there probably never even knew about this floating village hidden in the marshes.

All the way back to Meadows Road and at home that evening I felt strangely quiet. I knew, somehow, that I must keep the day's adventure a secret and that if I talked about it, everything would be spoiled. At supper I didn't even tell Sung Ge-ge anything. Y Jieh thought I was over-tired. I said nothing and went to bed safe with my secret thoughts of the day in the country. As I lay there, the cry of the curlews came back to me. 'Cour-lee, cour-lee.' I fell asleep wondering about them and remembering their distant lament.

□

'The first sorrowful mystery of the Holy Rosary, "The Agony in the Garden". . . .' My mother, dressed in black, was saying the rosary with us in our bedroom. Every night for a week now we had been mourning my father. How long would he burn in purgatory, I wondered, as the beads slipped through my fingers. 'Holy Mary, Mother of God, pray for us sinners now and at the hour of our death, amen.'

It was Brother Faust who had brought the news. First he had seen my mother, and she had rushed upstairs to her room, weeping. Then he had asked Pat and me to come into the drawing-room. 'My poor boys, you must pray to God for strength,' he said. 'Your father died suddenly in Shanghai yesterday. He collapsed on the road by the riverside. I believe it may have been sunstroke. A rickshaw coolie put him in his rickshaw and took him to the French convent of the Little Sisters of the Poor, not far away. The nuns laid him on a bench in their parlour and did all they could for him while they waited for an ambulance, but he died there before the ambulance arrived. You must do your best to comfort your poor mother.'

'The second sorrowful mystery, "The Crowning with Thorns". . . .'

My father had been away to Hankow and Shanghai so often that I had hardly seen him at all that year. 'Sure, I'll take you and Pat with me to the County Clare one day,' he would say to me in the Irish brogue my mother so disliked. Now that could never happen. In the days to come, I tried to keep a clear picture of my father, but his face began to fade and I was left only with vague memories of a tall stranger walking by the rickshaw coolies and pedlars on our street corner.

My father was buried in the French cemetery near the river in Shanghai. My mother was too upset to go to the funeral, but Brother Faust went. He brought back some photographs of the grave. It had a Celtic cross made of granite. Carved on it were the words 'Stephen Power. 1887 to 1925. R.I.P.' My mother wrote to my grandmother in Ireland and sent her one of the photographs.

In case the sorrowful mysteries of the rosary were not enough, I thought I had better say some more prayers for my father's soul. I searched my *Garden of the Soul* and found a list of prayers under the heading 'Plenary Indulgences'.

'Jesus meek and humble of heart, make my heart like unto Thine.'
300 days' indulgence each time.

'Jesus, Mary, Joseph I give you my heart and soul.'
    3 years each time.
'Lord have mercy on the souls in purgatory.'
    7 years and 7 quarantines each time.

In one night's praying alone, I saved my father from 360 years and 280 quarantines in purgatory. I kept it up for a few weeks and once or twice Y Jieh found me asleep on my knees.

One day, about four months after my father's funeral, a letter reached us from Ireland. It had been written by the scribe who lived near my father's old home at Querrin. Stephen's mother and father had received the photograph of his grave, the letter told us. A mass had been said for Stephen's soul. His mother was keeping strong despite her years and had been out helping with the harvest although the weather was terrible these last weeks. A cargo ship had run aground under the cliffs by Kilkee and had broken up on the rocks.

In the autumn following the long hot summer of 1925 when my father died, my sister Stephanie was born in the Victoria Hospital. When my mother came home with the baby, Pat and I moved downstairs to a room in the basement. The door to it lay in the passageway between the front garden and the backyard. The damp brick walls of our new room were unpainted and the small window had iron bars, so we nicknamed it the dungeon, but we liked the excitement of being on our own, close to the garden.

Famine followed the drought at the end of the autumn, and the peasants were on the move again. One day Sung Ge-ge brought an old hunchback into our backyard and gave him something to eat. Although he was about fifty years old, he was smaller than me. He never spoke, but sat on a bench and ate anything he was given.

The next day the hunchback was in the backyard again. Y Jieh gave him some odd jobs to do. At night he was allowed to sleep in a corner of the yard. We took care not to let my mother know for she would have been horrified. When the nights got colder, Pat said the hunchback could sleep on a piece of matting in a corner of our room. At bedtime Pat talked to him and made him laugh. We tried to find out where he had come from, but he would only say, '*Da ho.* . . . Big river,' and sit there with a grin on his face. He slept in his clothes, and reeked of garlic and stale sweat, but we enjoyed his company. Long before we woke up in the morning he would be gone, leaving his matting neatly rolled up. Sung Ge-ge said that he had found work on the bund as a coolie. In the evening he would help Y Jieh and then have supper with us.

One night he didn't come home. We kept his piece of neatly-rolled matting in case he should return, but we never saw him again.

□

Sung Ge-ge was practising 'Meeting a tiger half-way up the mountain' one day, and I was sitting on a chair watching him, when my mother sent for me. 'I want you to take this to the hotel and give it to Grandfather,' she said, handing me a letter. Grandfather d'Arc! I was so startled that I dropped the letter on the floor. 'There's no need to worry,' my mother went on. 'He'll be kind to you and it won't take long. But remember, don't let the Number One Boy take it from you. You're to give it to Grandfather yourself.'

I walked very slowly along the road, wishing Pat would appear and come to my rescue. Lucky Pat, he was always out when there was a message to deliver. The further I walked, the more frightened I became. I had only ever seen Grandfather in the distance at the Bastille Day parade.

Pat used to think he looked funny, but I felt overawed by this man who was a descendant of Joan of Arc, a hero of the French Army and the enemy of my father. Now I was on my way to meet him and my knees were knocking.

At All Saints Church I turned the corner into Racecourse Road. A hundred yards along, on the other side, was the Masonic Hall and next to it the grey stone fortress of d'Arc's Hotel. Trying hard to be brave, I pulled the bell-handle. The heavy wooden door with iron bars across it opened with a creak and a huge Number One Boy in a long gown appeared in the doorway. I clutched the letter tightly in case he should take it away, and asked to see my grandfather. He looked me up and down and I felt miserable. The sleeves of my jacket, which had been handed down from Pat, were far too long for me. One of my socks was hanging down and my shoes were covered in dust. He said nothing, but went on looking at me. Behind him, somewhere in the hall, a parrot began to squawk. 'I must see Master Dah-ke,' I repeated. At last he stood aside and beckoned me in.

The entrance hall was small and dark and filled with Chinese things. There were painted screens, lacquered tables, vases, clocks and a gong with a stick beside it. The whole place smelled strongly of furniture polish. On the right was a European-style leather sofa and two armchairs. In one of them an elderly foreign visitor sat reading a newspaper. He looked up for a moment and then went back to his paper.

Facing me, across the length of the hall, heavy curtains hung down to the floor. On my left, near the front door, a yellow and white cockatoo sat on a perch. When it saw me it jumped up and down, cackling with laughter and crying, '*Ni hao, ni hao*. . . . How do you do, how do you do.' Then it sat still again with its head on one side, watching me.

The Number One Boy signalled to me and I followed him across the hall to the curtains. As we reached them, the cockatoo screeched and cried out, '*Tai Tai! Tai Tai!* . . . Mistress! Mistress!' My face flushed. What if Grandmother should hear and come out to find me here! The Boy parted the curtain to reveal a door which he opened for me. I stepped through.

An amazing scene confronted me. Flags hung down from a low ceiling and the walls were covered with weapons and uniforms. I was standing in a battlefield. At the far end of the long room was an old black coach with two big wheels. Its long shafts lay on the ground. Small brass crowns decorated each corner of its roof. On the door was a brass letter N surrounded by a laurel wreath. Inside, the coach was lined with red leather.

Beside the coach, a man was sitting on a low straight-backed seat, covered with the same red leather. His bulging eyes stared at me through small gold-rimmed spectacles which were attached to his nose. His hair was iron grey and his big moustache was waxed at the ends. He wore a neatly-pressed black suit, a starched white collar and a grey cravat with a pearl. Smoke curled up from a cigar in his hand. A decanter of brandy and a half-filled glass stood on a round table near by.

Trembling all over, I walked up to him and held out the

letter. He took it from me without a word and opened it with a black paper-knife. As he glanced at the first page, he picked up his glass and sipped from it, taking care not to wet his moustache. He put the glass on the table. Without looking at the other pages, he folded them and returned them to the envelope.

'So you are Pat,' he said in a hoarse voice.

'No. Brian.'

'Oh, the second one.'

Feeling embarrassed, and afraid of meeting his eyes, I looked at some swords hanging on the wall.

'Those swords belonged to officers of the 1st Royal Dragoons. You are interested in weapons?'

I nodded.

'Do you know anything about the battle of the Taku forts which led to the capture of Tientsin by the French and the British?'

'Wang the park policeman told us a little about it, and Pat has a book . . .'

'Wang, eh? Well, never you mind what people or books tell you. Use your eyes, look around you. The whole of the battle for Tientsin is on these walls. There is no other collection in the world like this.'

Grandfather stood up. He put out his hand and lovingly caressed the side of the coach. 'This was given to General de Montauban, the French commander-in-chief, by the Emperor Napoleon III. But that was at the end of the battle. Come, let us start at the beginning.' We walked along the length of the wall carrying the weapons and uniforms of French and British regiments. Grandfather marched at a slow, stately pace as if he was leading a funeral cortège. Now and then he would halt to point out something, then our march continued.

We crossed the room to the Chinese wall. In the middle of it was a pole with a tattered yellow banner attached to it. On either side were spears and bows and arrows. Grandfather stopped before a gun about twelve feet long. 'A rampart rifle. The Chinese fired them at us from the Taku forts.' At the end of the wall, near the coach and grandfather's seat, was a cotton hood with black and yellow stripes painted on it. It had thin slits for eyes and pointed cat's ears. 'What is that?' I asked nervously. He looked at me sharply. 'A tiger's hood. Have you heard of the

secret society of the White Lotus?' I nodded. 'Well, they wore
those hoods to frighten their enemies. Ever since the time of
Genghis Khan they've been using them. Hoods or no hoods, the
Lotus behaved like tigers, moving by night, close to water.'

After our tour of the battlefield, Grandfather opened a small
iron safe behind his chair and took out a roll of Chinese dollar
bills. He counted some out, put them in an envelope and handed
it to me. 'Give this to your mother. Would you like to hear more
about the battle of Tientsin?' I nodded. 'Come back the same
time next week. You can go out by that door.' He pointed to a
small door behind the coach. 'It opens on to the stable-yard at
the back. There is an alleyway which leads into Racecourse
Road. When you come next week, knock on that door.'

I drew a bolt and opened the small back door. In the cobble-
stoned yard were some dusty old carriages. As I was closing the
door, I looked inside again. Grandfather had gone back to his
seat and was sitting there stiffly, looking straight ahead of him as
if he was a staff officer waiting by his commander-in-chief's
coach for orders. A feeling of pity for him came over me. His
puppet-like figure seemed even smaller than before. Looming
over him, the officers and men in scarlet and silver lined up for
battle against the men with spears and the yellow banner. The
black slits in the tiger's hood watched my grandfather patiently,
waiting for the right moment to make a savage leap.

In the coming weeks I went back to that strange battlefield
each Wednesday evening. I would stay for an hour and when I
left, Grandfather d'Arc would give me an envelope with money
in it for my mother. I no longer felt frightened of him. Instead,
even though he repeated himself a lot, I became more and more
fascinated by the stories he had to tell about the battles near
Tientsin during the Opium War.

□

Grandfather poured the last drop of brandy from the decanter
into his glass. 'Friendly allies?' he growled. 'The British and the
French? Hah! If only you knew. There were bitter quarrels
between them on every day of the campaign. What a row there
was over the ponies! The French artillery needed ponies to draw
their Napoleon guns, so the British offered to sell them 170 of

their surplus Indian ponies. But the price was too high and the French, who were not going to be cheated, had to send an officer to buy ponies from Japan.'

Usually he sipped his brandy slowly, but today Grandfather gulped it down. Reaching out his arm, he pulled the bell-handle on the wall. 'Then there was the victory parade in Tientsin where the Victoria Park is today. Do you think the Allies could agree on a date? Oh no! So two parades had to be held.' Reverently, he stroked the side of the black coach. 'Yes, this is the coach which carried General de Montauban at the French victory parade. But I've told you that already, haven't I? Yes. Well . . . you must stop me.'

The back door opened with a creaking noise and an old bald-headed coolie came in. His name was Wei, which meant 'guard'. There was a scar about two inches long on one side of his neck. Without looking at us, he shuffled to the table, picked up the decanter and carried it away.

Slumped in his chair, Grandfather began to mutter to himself. 'Opium. That was what poisoned the alliance. The British opium trade. We Frenchmen despised them for it. The Chinese tried to block it. But more and more came flooding in from India. Oh, they kept quiet about it, of course. There's not a word about opium in the Treaty of Tientsin. It's all in the customs tariff, hidden at the end of a long list of foreign imports. The Chinese Maritime Customs set up by the treaty and served by the Irish. They were the lot who ran the opium traffic.'

'*No offence intended, Steve.*' Like an echo, Brother Faust's words came back to trouble me once again. Vague memories of that scene in our drawing-room on St Patrick's eve had always started me wondering about my father. 'Do you think he kept an opium den?' I would ask Pat. But he only laughed and never answered me.

The door creaked and Wei returned with a full decanter. To my surprise, he gave me a friendly grin. It made me feel better and I stopped thinking about my father's secret opium den. Grandfather stood up. He walked slowly over to the Chinese wall and peered at the tattered yellow banner. 'They were trying to stop the British and the French from reaching Peking. It was the last battle fought by the Imperial Chinese Army. This banner was at the heart of it.' As he talked on, the rows of faded uniforms came to life again. With pennants hanging limply in the airless heat, they formed a ghostly procession winding along the dusty plain on the way to the Celestial City.

The French were leading the Allied column. Half-way to Peking, they came on an astonishing sight. Arrayed before them in ancient battle formation, was the Emperor's army. At the front were lines of Tartar horsemen. Behind them were the foot soldiers, flanked by archers armed with crossbows.

In the rear, visible from afar, a white marble bridge spanned a stream, a tributary of the Sea River. A giant Chinese warrior stood on the bridge, carrying the yellow banner.

The French prepared to attack, but it was the Chinese who made the first move. The lines of Tartar cavalry began to advance at the trot in close formation. From the bridge, the giant waved his banner to signal the orders of the Chinese general to all his men.

As they neared the French, the Tartar cavalry charged and were cut down by the Napoleon guns. De Montauban counter-attacked. His guns were moved up and their terrible fire was concentrated on the centre of the Chinese defence at the bridge. Although shells were exploding all around him, the giant stood defiantly at his post, waving the banner. Marvelling at his courage, and wishing to save him, de Montauban commanded his artillery to stop firing, but before the order could be carried out, a shell mortally wounded the giant. He sank slowly to his knees and then fell face forward across the floor of the bridge.

There was a long silence. Grandfather stood to attention before the banner on the wall. Then he took off his spectacles and wiped them carefully with a handkerchief. I felt I ought to say something.

'The French cannons in Victoria Park, Grandfather. Were they the ones used at the battle of the bridge?'

'Yes. One of them might have fired the shell that killed the giant flag-bearer.'

After the battle of the bridge, the Allied armies had Peking at their mercy. But, instead of entering the city, they turned westwards and raced each other for the glittering prize of the Summer Palace a few miles from Peking, where many of the Emperor's treasures were stored. Grandfather had reached the most dreadful part of his story.

The Imperial Summer Palace, with its pagodas and pavilions half-hidden by cedar trees, stood on the shore of a lake. When Sir Hope Grant, the British commander, entered the palace, he saw British and French of all ranks hurling each other out of the way and cursing as they fought savagely for the treasures. All discipline was forgotten and calls for order were ignored.

In his tent in the British camp that night, Captain Gordon of the Royal Engineers lay awake listening to the sound of chiming clocks and tinkling music-boxes coming from the soldiers' tents. It was like a nightmare. Unable to sleep, he began to write a letter home. 'Everyone was wild for plunder,' he wrote. 'It was a scene of utter destruction that passes my description.'

'I do not know if the British officers realized it,' said Grandfather, 'but among the things which they looted from the palace were presents which Lord Macartney had brought to the Emperor of China from the British monarch, King George III, in 1793. It was madness, utter madness! You see, we were playing into the hands of the Lotus. It suited them that the Manchu emperor should be forced to flee to his retreat in Jehol.'

Grandfather was silent for a time. Then he suddenly said, 'They will never catch the Yellow Lotus, you know. As soon as one dies, another takes her place.' He sat back, exhausted, in his red leather seat. His face, which had become inflamed, grew pale again. 'Madness, utter madness,' he repeated as he stared at the wall on which hung the swords of the French and the British.

Behind him, on the Chinese wall, the black slits in the tiger's hood gave no sign when or how the masked men would strike.

□

'*Memento homo quia pulvis es.* . . . Remember man that thou art dust, and unto dust thou shalt return.' As he spoke the words of the psalm, Father Molinari scattered some earth on Grandfather d'Arc's coffin lying deep in its grave. Then Grandmother and my mother each threw some earth on the coffin. Father Molinari took the thurible from the acolyte and incensed the grave. He said a last prayer, then, followed by the small group of mourners, he walked away towards the gate of the French cemetery. He had buried his black sheep. Only death had brought my grandfather's body back to the church, and then only for the last rites.

I waited in the light drizzle to watch two coolies throwing spadefuls of wet yellow earth into the grave. At first the earth made loud thuds as it struck the coffin. Then, as the grave filled, it fell silently. What a pity, I thought, that Grandfather had not had a military funeral. I had expected to see a detachment of French soldiers firing their rifles over his grave, but there had not even been an old comrade from the Legion of Frontiersmen to salute him.

All my mother could tell me about Grandfather's death was that he had had a heart attack. One day I went round to the back entrance of d'Arc's Hotel and saw Wei, the old coolie. He was the last person to see Grandfather alive. In the morning Grandfather had been sitting in his red leather seat as usual. When the coolie next saw him, he was lying on the ground, facing the Chinese wall. In his right hand was the tiger's hood. He was gripping it so tightly that the coolie could not free it.

As Wei talked on, I no longer listened to what he was saying, for I could see in vivid detail what had happened and did not need to be told. Staring into the menacing eyes of the tiger, Grandfather must have thought it was about to spring on him, so he had rushed forward to grapple with it. Somehow, from my very first visit to that strange arena hidden behind the curtains, I had always known that this would happen.

'You died on your battlefield after all, Grandfather,' I whispered on the way home. The thought made me glad for his sake and I forgot the misery of his drab funeral when no flag, no bugle call and no shot had honoured him.

VI

The first dust storm of spring was blowing when a company of Japanese soldiers, many of them wearing face-masks, cordoned off all the approaches to Tientsin railway station. On the arrival platform for the train from Peking, a group of specially invited foreigners and Chinese dignitaries waited with the Japanese Consul-General. Among them on this historic occasion was Mr Woodhead of the *Peking and Tientsin Times*.

The train was late. The old lantern at the end of the platform had already been lit when, in the distance, the train's long and melancholy whistle was heard. The station-master's handbell clanged out its warning and the train came in, panting and hissing. A guard of honour presented arms, trumpeters sounded a fanfare, and everyone removed their hats and bowed as a frail young man of twenty descended the steep steps. He wore a long black Manchu gown, a black skull-cap and large black-rimmed spectacles. A bamboo cane hung on his left arm. When he walked along the front rank of the guard of honour, his arms and legs jerked as if he was a puppet dangling on the end of strings. Pu Yi, once Dragon Emperor of China, had come to the Ford of Heaven.

When greetings had been exchanged, the former emperor was driven in a motor car, one of the earliest seen in Tientsin, to a large house in the Japanese Concession which was to be his new home. It was called the Quiet Garden.

Recently, an attempt to restore Pu Yi to the throne in Peking had been thwarted by the war-lord Feng Yu Hsiang and his Bolshevik supporters. Fearing for his life, Pu Yi had gone to the Japanese for protection and they had offered him refuge in Tientsin.

The foreign press gave the august new resident a warm welcome. Most of the papers had supported the treacherous pretender Yuan Shi Kai, but after his sudden death they shifted their allegiance to Pu Yi and were now all staunch supporters of the movement to restore the Manchu dynasty of the Ching. 'Republicanism in China has been tried and found wanting,' proclaimed the *North China Daily Mail*. 'The mercantile classes and the gentry of China are weary of it. A coup d'état should be brought off, for we all know that nothing succeeds like success.'

Those members of the imperial entourage, officers, eunuchs and concubines, who had fled when the Ching dynasty fell in 1911, now came cringing back to worship the Son of Heaven at the Quiet Garden where he held court. Very soon foreign soldiers of fortune also presented themselves at the Quiet Garden with offers of military help in exchange for cash. One day a large American car with its headlights full on and its horn blaring, raced from the Russian Concession through the Italian Concession and crossed the Austrian bridge to the south side of the river. Men in overcoats, brandishing revolvers, stood on the car's running-boards as it roared at high speed towards the Japanese Concession. In the rear seat, half hidden by his bodyguard, a Cossack general leaned back, smoking a cigar. The ogre Semenov had arrived in Tientsin.

The car stopped with a screech of brakes outside the Quiet Garden. Semenov was shown into Pu Yi's presence. He offered Pu Yi his private army of mercenaries to restore the Ching dynasty. Pu Yi, short of cash, was embarrassed. Would Semenov accept some of the imperial jewels to make up the balance? Semenov agreed. A formal pact was then signed. It was called the 'Sino-Russian Anti-Bolshevik Convention'.

Sitting on one side of Pu Yi's reception room during that meeting was a man whom Semonov probably scarcely noticed. A thickset Japanese with a shaven head, he wore a drab-looking grey civilian suit such as a junior official might possess. He seemed not to be paying much attention to the proceedings, but every now and then his black reptilian eyes would dart a look at Semenov and then return to hide beneath their hooded lids. This was Colonel Doihara of the Japanese secret service.

Foreigners in Peking and Shanghai, who had long been in the

habit of looking down on the squalid inland port on the Sea River, now envied Tientsin its new-found status of imperial refuge. Hardly a day passed without the papers writing in their social columns about their favourite subject, the young ex-emperor. He attended the ceremony of Trooping the Colour at the British barracks on the King's birthday and he was piped on board HMS *Hollyhock* at the bund. The British Country Club, which had a strict rule against admitting any Chinese, passed an amendment granting Pu Yi membership as a 'special Chinese'.

But of all Tientsin's residents, none were more delighted by the ex-emperor's arrival than the Scottish colony. At first Pu Yi went about in his gown and skull-cap, but he soon took to wearing clothes which a gentleman might wear in Edinburgh. At the St Andrew's Day ball in the Astor House he wore a white tie and tails. At the golf club, where he was made an honorary member, he was photographed in a tweed jacket, plus-fours and flat cap.

Pu Yi's passion for Scottish customs had begun early in life. During his boyhood in the Forbidden Palace, he had had for a tutor Mr Reginald Johnston, a Scot who had been an official in the British Consular Service. According to a courtier, Mr Johnston had looked on with a patronizing smile when, one day, the boy emperor said he would like to have a tartan for the imperial household. If Queen Victoria's consort Prince Albert could design a tartan, why can't I? Pu Yi pleaded. And why should we not have a Chinese kilted pipe band playing in the grounds of the Forbidden Palace? At this, the smile on Mr Johnston's face had faded to be replaced by a look of alarm.

The climax of Pu Yi's social round came with the visit to Tientsin of His Royal Highness the Duke of Gloucester. The royal Duke paid a courtesy call at the Quiet Garden. Pu Yi presented him with a photograph of himself and received in exchange one of King George and Queen Mary of England.

Hovering in the wings at these events was the thickset man with the shaven head. He would stand behind a pillar of the ballroom in the Astor House or walk at a steady pace on the golf course. Whenever Pu Yi was photographed, this man in grey would be in the picture, usually to one side. No one bothered to pay any attention to him, for he seemed to be just part of the background.

The ex-emperor had hardly been in Tientsin for a year when
people found out that Colonel Doihara was more than a
bodyguard and adviser to Pu Yi. The Japanese secret service-
man's real mission was to hunt down members of the secret
society of the White Lotus. Of all the anti-Ching movements, it
was the most dangerous. He worked closely with the British
Municipal Council's Watch Committee and soon became
recognized as the effective head of intelligence work against the
Lotus in Tientsin.

Within a short time Colonel Doihara made some important
discoveries. The leaders of the Lotus worked in small cells of
about five or six people. Each cell specialized in a different task:
guiding migrant peasants across Tientsin by night, providing
them with food and shelter, smuggling salt, and raiding ships
and godowns for foodstuffs. One day, when the time was ripe for
overthrowing the regime in Peking, the cells would come
together and form the spearhead for a general rising of the
peasants.

'A real breakthrough,' said Woodhead of the *Peking and
Tientsin Times*. 'Colonel Doihara is the Lawrence of the East.'

□

'The smallest garrisons of soldiers make the loudest noise,' was
an old saying among the Chinese. 'Cheeky devils!' said Captain
O'Riordan when I translated it for him one day. 'But there's
truth in it, of course.'

All the foreign garrisons were small, for their forces were
stretched from Hong Kong in the south to Manchuria in the
north. To make up for their lack of numbers, they showed the
flag, and their parades had been a feature of life in the
Concessions since the earliest days.

'There's nothing like the sight of a well-drilled regiment for
keeping the natives quiet,' said Captain O'Riordan, when he
and his wife were having tea with us one Sunday.

'I hear that the Watch Committee is now being run by
Colonel Doihara,' my mother said. 'Do you think you'll catch
any of the Lotus soon?'

'Quare fellow, that Jap. But he's the cleverest fox in town, I'll
wager.' The Captain dropped his voice. 'This is for your ears

only, you understand. We're expecting to make an arrest any day now. A foreigner, an American journalist, I believe. I'll say no more than that.' With a knowing look, he changed the subject. 'You can't help admiring the Japs. They've turned out to be our most trustworthy ally.'

Mrs O'Riordan, who had been smiling and nodding, forgot herself and suddenly said, 'Don't you think it's a compliment to us that the Japanese Consul lives in the British Concession in that fine house across the road from the cenotaph?'

The Captain ignored her and went on, 'All their top military commanders were trained in England, you know. They copy everything we do.'

On the Emperor of Japan's birthday Pat and I went to watch the parade in the Japanese park. Hundreds of little flags, white with a red sun in the middle, decorated the road which ran through the park. The Japanese troops looked grimly serious as they formed up. When the order for the imperial salute was given, the troops presented arms and the Japanese children waved their rising sun flags as they all shouted, '*Tenno Banzai*!' Just then, three Japanese airforce planes flew low over our heads, making a big roar. They were the first aeroplanes I had ever seen. Each plane had two sets of wings. You could see the red sun markings on the planes and the pilots' heads sticking out of the cockpits.

We were leaving the park with the crowd after the parade when a cordon of police pushed us back on to the pavement to make way for a procession of important motor cars. The first was full of officers. An open car followed, surrounded by soldiers on motor cycles. A thin young man was standing in the front of this car. He wore a military cap with white plumes on it. One of the plumes hung down and touched his spectacles. Looking bewildered, he raised his hand to his cap in salute, but no one seemed to take much notice of him. It was Pu Yi, once emperor of all China.

□

One afternoon when the band was playing in Victoria Park, I met Helen Gable, the girl with the golden hair, again. We sat on a bench in silence for a long time. Then, as I got up to go, she invited me to tea at her home on the following Sunday. It was to be the first of several visits.

Captain Gable of the 15th United States Infantry and Mrs Gable lived in Woodrow Wilson Street in the former German Concession. Every Sunday, about twenty people would gather at their house. Mrs Gable was an ardent fund raiser for an American Protestant sect. She was much taller than her husband, a mild man with sandy hair and freckles, who always called his wife 'the boss'.

The party would begin with some rollicking tunes played on gramophone records while Helen handed round cups of tea and biscuits which she called 'cookies'. There was hardly ever time to speak to her, even when I could think of something to say.

'I guess the boss would like our family anthem now!' cried Captain Gable. Everyone laughed and clapped as he put on Mrs Gable's favourite gramophone record.

> 'California! Here I come,
> Right back where I started from,
> Open up, open up those pearly gates,
> California! Here I come.'

After this light entertainment, there came a hush as Mrs Gable, in a sombre mood, seated herself at the piano. 'The boss and I would like you to join with us in our mission hymn,' Captain Gable said softly. 'Maybe this is a good moment to remember that all over America folks will be meeting in aid of the China mission and singing these same words.'

> 'Give of thy sons to bear the message glorious,
> Give of thy wealth to speed them on their way.
> Pour out thy soul for them in prayer victorious,
> And all thou spendest Jesus will repay.'

During the hymn, Helen looked at me appealingly from across the room. Was she trying to convert me to her mother's sect·or was she begging me to rescue her from it? I never could tell.

On Monday mornings, back in the Catholic world of St Louis, I carefully avoided catching Brother Paul's eye. He always seemed to know when I had been to one of the Gables' Protestant tea parties. Once, when I was day-dreaming about Helen during essay writing, I looked up to find Brother Paul standing beside me. It was impossible to hide my blushes.

Captain Gable's regiment was nicknamed the 'Can Do's' after the pidgin English spoken by the American soldiers to their coolies. The Americans were the highest-paid soldiers in Tientsin, so they could afford to employ coolies to clean their quarters and perform other menial tasks. A hierarchy of Number One Boys supervised the coolies. Captain O'Riordan disapproved of soldiers having servants. It was bad for discipline and security. 'Mark my words,' he said, 'they'll have the coolies cleaning their rifles for them next!'

On American Independence Day the Can Do's always staged a mock battle in period dress at their parade ground. I was thrilled when Helen Gable invited me to go to the parade with her. We had seats in the stand where the officers from all the foreign garrisons were assembled.

The 'battle' began with the deafening noise of crackers exploding. At this, many Chinese came running up from the nearby streets to swell the crowds already watching the performance. George Washington, mounted on a Mongolian pony, led his men into the attack against a regiment of British Redcoats. At the height of the battle, the Redcoats turned and ran, chased by the Americans. In the visitors' stand, the British officers smiled their thin polite smiles, while the French chuckled with obvious delight. The Japanese officers looked on at the charade without any expressions on their faces at all.

I was escorting Helen home after the performance when she suddenly clutched my arm. 'I'm sorry about the British losing,' she said. 'I guess they didn't have a chance, wearing that gaudy uniform.'

I felt very moved. Whether it was her sympathetic words or the way she pressed my arm, I couldn't say, but the daring thought entered my mind that one day soon I would ask her to go with me to the pictures at the Empire Cinema.

□

The Empire Cinema was a favourite haunt of the Siberian boys from St Louis. On Saturday afternoons the performance always began with the same ritual. Herr Schneider, who looked so like Charlie Chaplin, would walk down the five steps into the orchestra pit, take his violin out of its case and rest it on a small pad on his shoulder. The pianist would sound the key note while Herr Schneider tuned his strings. After bowing to the cellist and second violin who made up the rest of the quartet, Herr Schneider would turn to glance up at the cinema manager who stood beside the film projector at the back of the gallery. It was his signal for the picture to begin and we settled down in our seats to watch yet another instalment of the serial *Tarzan of the Apes*.

The lights were put out and, to the accompaniment of eerie music from the orchestra, Tarzan, the English aristocrat who had been brought up in the jungle and understood the language of animals, rode into view sitting on the back of an African elephant with a small chimpanzee perched on his shoulder. Behind Tarzan, on a smaller elephant, rode his wife Jane and their child.

The tempo of the music quickened when Tarzan's enemies appeared. They were usually traders or hunters on safari. Whenever Tarzan was in danger, all the elephants and apes would come running to his rescue. There seemed no end to Tarzan's adventures. Just as we thought that the picture was reaching its climax, the dismal words 'To be continued next week' would be flashed on the screen and we were left frustrated as we watched the orchestra put away their instruments.

When, at last, the serial neared its end and the screen turned a pink colour to show that the forest was in flames, Herr Schneider did not spare himself. He played with such passionate fury that the cinema itself seemed to catch fire.

You could tell what Herr Schneider thought of a film by the way he played. He was at his best in the short Charlie Chaplin pieces when he would put all his heart into his playing. I sometimes wondered if he was living the role Charlie played on the screen, as he plucked briskly at his strings in the funny parts of the story and drew his bow gently over them in the sad parts.

Many of the pictures we saw were about cowboys and Indians in the American Wild West. Herr Schneider did not care for them. The plot never changed and there was little he and his orchestra could do with the same old saloon-bar scenes and the endless galloping of the horses. But there was another reason why Herr Schneider disliked the cowboy pictures. Pat, Kravchuk and Ibragimoff took to throwing down paper darts from the front row of the gallery. The cowboy pictures always brought out the worst in them. On two or three occasions they scored a direct hit on Herr Schneider when he was playing. The cinema manager did his best to catch the missile throwers, but it was a long time before he succeeded.

One afternoon, a cowboy picture reached its inevitable climax. Brave American settlers, guarded by a troop of Rangers, were being besieged in their stockade. The Red Indians had just lit smoke signals in the surrounding hills as an order to attack, when a shower of paper darts sailed down into the orchestra pit. The music stopped. Angry voices could be heard in the pit and chuckles in the gallery. Suddenly the lights came on and the cinema manager rushed forward. Ibragimoff was caught, but Pat and Kravchuk managed to escape. Ibragimoff had his name taken and was forbidden to enter the cinema for a year.

It was scenes like those which made me think again about asking Helen to the pictures. The Siberians from my school were bound to see me with her, and even if they didn't tease me in the cinema, I knew I hadn't the courage to face them in school on Monday.

When talking pictures came to the Empire Cinema, it became a much less exciting place. The new films were all alike with booming music and drawling voices recorded on the sound-track. In each of them, it seemed, glamorous stars were driven endlessly in big automobiles to grand hotels.

The orchestra pit was now a silent and empty cave. Gone were the stirring tones of Herr Schneider's violin. Three dusty old music stands remained in a corner of the pit for some time. One day I noticed that they had been cleared away and I realized then that the orchestra would never return. I missed them very much.

Herr Schneider went on playing in the trio at Kiessling's, but the familiar Viennese waltzes, drowned by the chatter of voices, did not ask so much of his artistry as the exciting cinema music. I always felt that he might have been a fine concert performer. Once, when Chaliapin, the Russian singer, came to Tientsin

during his world tour and gave a concert at Gordon Hall, I
turned round in my seat and saw Herr Schneider in the row
behind, weeping silently.

The Empire Cinema was usually packed with soldiers on
Friday evenings because it was their pay-day. When the
programme ended, hordes of soldiers walked down to the
drinking bars and brothels in nearby Dublin Road.

Mad Mac and Captain O'Riordan had one of their worst
quarrels over the brothels or 'bad houses' as my mother called
them. 'Our soldiers look smart enough on parade,' said Mad
Mac, 'but they are just a drunken rabble when they are let loose
in Dublin Road. Even their own military police can't stop them
fighting outside the brothels.'

'It's the Americans' fault,' said the Captain, shaken by this
onslaught. 'They're so highly paid, the prostitutes . . .'

'Steady on, I must ask you . . . not in front of the boys,' said
Brother Faust. But the argument had become too heated and he
was ignored.

'And what about the V D?' Mad Mac asked. 'They'll tell you
at the Pasteur Institute that the epidemic of syphilis among the
foreign troops here is out of control.'

Mrs O'Riordan was in tears and my mother had to lead her
out of the room. If only my father had been here, I thought, he
would have been able to cheer everyone up. But the evening
ended in a deep gloom.

□

The most impressive British parade took place on the morning of
November 11, Armistice Day. It was held at the cenotaph in
Victoria Park and was modelled on the service in Whitehall,
London.

The Consul-General took the place of the king. A company of
British soldiers, sailors from HMS *Hollyhock*, the Volunteer
Corps, members of the British Legion and the Boy Scouts were
drawn up on three sides of the cenotaph. On the fourth side
stood the Consul-General, the chairman and members of the
British Municipal Council and, behind them, foreign military
guests in a variety of uniforms. There were French in blue-grey
steel helmets, Italians with bright blue sashes and gold

epaulettes, and Americans with wide-brimmed stetson hats.

The Japanese had long curved swords. They wore white masks over their mouths, a sign that the winter dust storms had begun. As they arrived to take their places, the foreign officers bowed to each other and saluted with much ceremony. Once I saw an American officer skip out of the way just in time as a long Japanese sword swung round and nearly tripped him up.

British families, well wrapped up in furs against the cold weather, gathered behind the soldiers while crowds of curious Chinese watched from outside the railings. This was a big day for Wang, who strode proudly about the park like a captain on his ship.

The procession of clergy and choirboys, which had walked from All Saints Church, arrived at the cenotaph at exactly ten minutes to eleven. The vicar of All Saints, wearing his Master of Arts hood round his neck, conducted the service, assisted by several Protestant missionaries. There were no Catholic priests or religious brothers present. I took care not to join in the singing. Brother Paul said it was a sin to take part in a Protestant service because their ministers were not real priests.

> 'O God our help in ages past,
> Our hope for years to come,
> Our shelter from the stormy blast,
> And our eternal home. . . .'

The thin, sad wailing of the women mingled with the flute-like voices of the choirboys and the rough flat voices of the men as they sang their mournful hymn. The vicar read some prayers in a faltering voice. Brother Paul was right, I thought, there could be no miracle at a service like this as there was in the mass.

Suddenly a bugle rang out from the ramparts of Gordon Hall, sounding the Last Post. The two minutes' silence began for those who had fallen in the Great War in Europe. My mother sniffed and dabbed at her eyes with a handkerchief. Was she remembering her German friends? Once, the Germans and the British had been allies and they had fought side by side against the Boxers. Just across the road, by the Tientsin Club, you could see where Victoria Road joined what used to be Kaiser Wilhelm Strasse. Now the name had been altered to Woodrow Wilson

Street. How quickly allies changed into enemies!

More bugles sounded the Reveille and, as the band started to play Chopin's funeral march, the Consul-General laid his wreath of poppies at the foot of the cenotaph, followed by the other officials and officers. When all the wreaths had been laid, the parade marched off, led by the band playing 'It's a Long Way to Tipperary'. This was Wang's favourite tune and he jerked his arm up and down, beating time as the parade went by.

The civic dignitaries and officers saluted each other and went their different ways. Captain O'Riordan turned to Mrs O'Riordan and my mother. 'Well, didn't that go well?' he said. 'Clockwork precision! You've got to give us credit. The British know how to run a ceremonial parade better than anyone else.' At the park gate we squeezed past Wang who was standing there in his huge overcoat with brass buttons, still beating time to the tune of 'Tipperary' as if he was the bandmaster.

Facing Gordon Hall and overlooking the cenotaph, the flag of the Rising Sun on the Japanese Consul's house fluttered in the bitterly cold wind blowing from Mongolia. Winter was on its way.

VII

All winter long, from November to February, the cold winds blew from the Interior. The river and the canals and creeks froze. Everything was still. One by one, the pedlars disappeared to hide like moths in secret places, until only the tea pedlar was left at our corner. By Christmas-time even he had gone.

On Boxing Day a carnival was always held at the ice-skating rink. The first item on the programme was a fancy dress parade for children. My mother was determined that one of us should win it and she put all her imagination into designing the oddest of costumes for us. One year she decided that I was to be a Christmas tree. On the day of the carnival I had to stand in the middle of the bedroom while the elaborate process of dressing me went on. First I was sewn into a green felt garment. Then prickly fir branches were fixed onto it so that they stuck out in all directions. Lastly, tinsel, glass globes, stars and crackers were hung all over me. Barely able to see through my decorations, I was propped into a rickshaw and taken to the rink. But, by the time I had put on my skates and stepped on to the ice, we discovered that the fancy dress parade had just ended. Furious, my mother went to see the carnival committee. Fearing what she might do, and perhaps feeling a little sorry for me when they saw me under my branches, the committee came to a compromise and its chairman, Mr Peebles, made an announcement over the loudspeaker. 'Ladies and gentlemen, we are sure you will not want to miss seeing Mrs Power's son Brian in his remarkable costume. He will now skate once round the rink.'

A gramophone played the Viennese waltz 'Gold and Silver' and off I went, blushing with embarrassment and skating very slowly with my arms outstretched in case any of my decorations

107

should drop off. The corners of the rink were the worst part and twice I nearly fell. Somehow, I reached the committee box where my proud mother was standing. Mr Peebles presented me with a consolation prize of a box of chocolates and the audience clapped. My ordeal was over for another year.

Pat and I often went skating on the Hidden Creek. Once or twice we skated as far as the terminus of the Grand Canal where the monument to Khubilai Khan stood like a tall tombstone among some ruins. The few people we saw there were huddled together in their icebound boats.

Winter was a bad time for the water people. When they had no food, they were forced to bring their young daughters into the Concessions where they tried to sell them. Mrs O'Riordan and my mother thought that the Chinese were callous about their daughters, but I knew that was not true. Y Jieh said the families who lived in boats grieved over the loss of their young girls. She used to hum an old song of the canal people while Jieh-jieh sang the words:

> 'The north wind came in the night,
> Ice covers the waters.
> Once our young sister has gone
> She will never return.'

In the middle of the winter someone brought news that Cheng, the old boatman, had died. Y Jieh went to the canal district to help her friends. She was away for nearly a week.

With the coming of spring, the waters broke free of the ice, and the pedlars were on the street corner again. Jieh-jieh would celebrate by singing a little song on the way to the market.

Like migrating birds, the story-tellers returned. One day the Fool performed a mime I had not seen before. He played the parts of a Buddhist monk, a Confucian scholar and a hermit in the wild mountains who followed the Tao, the Way. After each part, he quickly changed his clothes which he kept in a cotton shoulder-bag.

First came the Buddhist monk. Dressed in flowing robes, he walked up and down with a mincing step while he rattled his beads. Now and again he would halt and, giving the audience a sly look, he would draw a begging bowl from inside his wide sleeve and hold it out for alms. Next came the Confucian sage who strutted about in a tall square-topped hat and gown. Full of pomp, he unfurled a long scroll and muttered as he read it. Both these characters made the crowd laugh with delight. Then, sweeping off the hat and gown, and wearing only the tattered rags of a peasant, the Fool seized a Taoist staff and pretended he was climbing a mountain. The crowd continued to laugh. Suddenly, the Taoist hermit turned and made a menacing lunge; the bamboo staff had became a spear! There was complete silence. Even the stall-holders and the pedlars stopped their cries and watched. Fear, excitement and anarchy were in the air.

Y Jieh said little about the Taoists, but she did tell me that Tao meant, simply, a road. I knew this was true for Jieh-jieh had shown me that the character for Tao was the same as the character for a road. The Tao also meant the Way, the way of nature. The Taoists had only one commandment, 'Do nothing against nature.' Their hermits lived in the mountains and laughed at people in the valleys and plains.

Although Y Jieh never went to a temple or a pagoda, I came to realize that she was a follower of the Way. She taught Jieh-jieh some ancient Taoist sayings which Jieh-jieh wrote down in characters:

The Tao flows everywhere and nourishes all things, but it does not try to possess them or rule over them.

Water is the noblest of the elements. It gives life to everything, yet it is humble and flows in those places which people despise. That is why water is so close to the Tao.

When, solemn-eyed, Jieh-jieh read them out in her quiet voice, I would think of limbo and the eternal beauty of its pale blue mountains.

□

Dull booming sounds, like a big drum being beaten, woke us up early one morning. After each boom the windows rattled. My mother came into our room, clutching her dressing-gown at the waist and shivering. 'They're firing cannons,' she said. 'It's coming from somewhere near the French Concession, I think. It must be Wu Pei Fu's army.'

For the past month Wu Pei Fu, the war-lord from central China, had been moving troops northwards. The Ford of Heaven was an important prize. All railway lines to Peking came through the town, and the railway yards were filled with reserve engines and coaches. Trains were as vital to the war-lords as horses had been to the Mongols. Not only did they move their armies by train, but they often lived with their concubines in first-class coaches which were lavishly furnished.

Feng Yu Hsiang, a rival war-lord but occasional ally of Wu Pei Fu, kept a piano in his private coach at Tsing Yuan, a hundred miles south-west of Peking, on the edge of the desert. Mad Mac had been out to tune it several times, and had struck up a friendship with the White Russian pianist who entertained the war-lord and his guests after dinner.

It was always risky to travel by train, even on the short journey of eighty miles to Peking. You might be stopped by bandits or by the troops of a war-lord. The few bedraggled republican soldiers who served as train guards were not much protection. As for the government, based far away in Nanking, it was powerless to prevent the feuding between rival war-lords who found arms easy to come by, especially after the end of the Great War in Europe when shiploads of surplus weapons arrived for sale in China.

The treacherous Wu Pei Fu's objective on this occasion was a train loaded with Italian arms in a siding east of Tientsin station. It was due to leave shortly for Tsing Yuan where Feng Yu Hsiang was waiting to take delivery.

If Wu Pei Fu wanted to seize any trains from Tientsin, he knew he would have to fight for them, because Chang Tso Lin, the Manchurian war-lord, considered Tientsin to be part of his domain. One of Chang's allies, General Liu Ching Li, had his headquarters near Tientsin. My mother called him the 'good war-lord' for he was supposed to be pro-British. It would have been truer to call him pro-Japanese, for both he and his chief Chang Tso Lin were in the pay of the Japanese High Command.

Mrs O'Riordan came to tea. In her trembling voice, she said

that the Captain was of the opinion that if H M S *Foxglove* didn't sail up the Sea River soon to reinforce the *Hollyhock*, then Tientsin was doomed. 'I'm sure Liu Ching Li's men will run away and desert us,' my mother kept saying as she paced up and down the room. That night I lay in bed and imagined men and women of the secret society of the White Lotus hiding in a long barge which came silently up the Grand Canal. Disguised as fishermen and coolies, they were stealing into Tientsin while the battle for the station was going on.

Although many people were worried by the siege, Y Jieh did not think that anything terrible was going to happen, and the pedlars came to our corner as usual.

'Wu Pei Fu's army closing in!' The *Peking and Tientsin Times* prepared us for the worst. British soldiers in steel helmets patrolled the Concession's boundaries. The Volunteer Corps was called up. Recruited from businessmen of various nationalities who lived in the British Concession, this force was the successor to the Legion of Frontiersmen which had long since been disbanded. Dressed in ill-fitting khaki uniforms and armed with an odd assortment of weapons, they stood guard at key positions like Gordon Hall and the Tientsin Club. Every evening my mother asked us if we had seen H M S *Foxglove* at the bund. And when Pat said he had seen her anchored round a bend of the river, she was not sure whether to believe him or not.

Train services to and from Tientsin were stopped. All berths on passenger ships leaving Tientsin were fully booked as the wives and children of the wealthier foreign families began to leave for places like Hong Kong. From there they would go on to England, France or America.

One day a rickshaw coolie brought me a note from Helen Gable. 'Please meet me in Victoria Park tomorrow afternoon.' That was all, but the words, the first she had ever written to me, became a passionate love letter as I read and re-read them with mounting excitement. Had she decided to run away from home? Did she want me to rescue her? I could hardly wait for the hours to pass, but I did my best to appear calm in case Pat should find out my secret.

On my way to the park I made my brave decision. Today I would ask Helen to the pictures. This time nothing would put me off, not even the thought of Kravchuk himself sitting in the row behind us and the things he and his gang might do when the lights came on!

I was leaning against the cannon by Wang's bench when Helen arrived. She was carrying a big white rabbit in her arms.

'Ma and I are leaving on a Japanese ship tomorrow.'

'Where are you going?'

'Yokohama. Then on a liner to California.'

'California! Here I come, Right back where I started from! . . ,' the ditty raced in my head.

'What's the matter?' Helen asked.

'Oh, nothing. Will you come back?'

'Pa says he will send for us when the troubles are over.'

'Well, goodbye.'

'I'd like you to have this,' she said, dumping the white rabbit in my arms.

On the way home, the rabbit felt heavier and heavier. Sung Ge-ge put it in a crate in the backyard. In the morning Y Jieh asked me to go down. My rabbit had produced a litter of twelve. Soon there were rabbits scampering all about the yard.

In future, whenever I heard the tune 'California', I would think of Helen and her rabbits. Had she realized how big a farewell present she had given me?

□

The intermittent sound of guns booming went on for several days and then stopped. There were conflicting reports from the battlefield and it wasn't until sometime later that we discovered what had happened. While the armies of Wu Pei Fu and Liu Ching Li faced each other and exchanged artillery fire, a group of men coupled an engine to the Italian arms train and made off down a branch line. They abandoned the train a mile from Tsing Yuan station.

By the time Feng Yu Hsiang found his train, its entire cargo had vanished. No one was in any doubt as to who the train robbers were. Only the White Lotus could have planned and carried out such a daring operation.

Meanwhile, seeing his prize vanish, Wu Pei Fu ordered his army to retreat. Cut off from their comrades, some pathetic remnants of Wu Pei Fu's men wandered aimlessly towards the

British racecourse. They were mistaken for an invading force and the cry went up, 'Racecourse under attack!'

The Can Do's were ordered to intercept them. Led by an officer on a pony, they marched to the racecourse. There they saw a miserable sight. A leaderless rabble of exhausted soldiers, many of them mere boys, sat on the ground. Some distance away, wounded men limped towards them while others lay in bloody rags on carts pulled by peasants who had been press-ganged from a village on the outskirts of Tientsin. Apart from the wounded men, the carts were piled high with pots and pans, all stolen from the peasants.

Eagerly, Wu Pei Fu's boy soldiers handed over their rifles to the Can Do's and snatched at the food they were offered. Afterwards many of them were absorbed into Liu Ching Li's army. Some of the maimed joined the professional beggars who roamed the streets.

There was a feeling of relief in Tientsin and, after the order to stand down, the Volunteers held a celebration party.

The grateful Chinese officials from the native quarter presented the Can Do's with a model of a gateway carved in ivory. From now on, this symbol of the defence of Tientsin was displayed on important occasions at Can Do Field, the American parade ground.

A story spread among the Chinese in the Concession that the ivory gateway had been intended for the invading war-lord Wu Pei Fu, should he have succeeded in capturing Tientsin station. If the story was true, then the Chinese officials who attended the big parades at Can Do Field betrayed no sign of it, not even by the faintest of smiles, as they sat near the ivory trophy at the saluting base and watched the troops marching past.

□

Walking back from the market with Y Jieh one morning, I saw that the sky in the west had turned a yellow colour. I asked Y Jieh about it, but she did not seem concerned and said nothing.

A wind began to blow. By midday the sky was yellow overhead and the wind was much stronger. Then the dust reached us. It swirled about everywhere and got into your eyes and mouth. We had to stay in the house and it was so dark that we put the lights on. From our bedroom window, I watched the pedlars pack up their things and carry them away on their shoulder-poles as fast as they could go. One or two rickshaw coolies remained behind, but after a time they, too, ran off.

The sky grew darker and darker and the wind howled until I thought it was going to blow down the umbrella tree. My mother came into our room. 'It's like the end of the world,' she said, her bottom lip trembling. Then Y Jieh came upstairs and told us not to be frightened. The strong west wind was bringing sand from the Gobi desert as it had always done. Soon it would die down.

I watched Y Jieh as she stood at the window. While she was looking out at the yellow sky, a mysterious thing happened. Her lined and weather-beaten face became young again and she smiled as though she was in league with the furious storm.

At bedtime we offered up prayers to the Little Flower for her help, but all through them I could think only of Y Jieh's face. Why did the sight of the dust from the big desert make her so happy? I never spoke to anyone about this, for something told me it should be kept secret.

All night and all the next day the dust storm raged. Then in the evening the wind quietened as Y Jieh said it would, and the sky in the west turned green and then back to blue.

After the storm our garden was covered with yellow sand and there were piles of dust in the street. How empty our street corner was without any pedlars! They did not return for a long time.

□

Just after dawn one spring morning when the brown reeds hardly stirred in the mist, old Cheng untied his sampan and we slipped away silently from the line of boats in the canal. At last we were going on our promised journey to the sea.

Cheng stood in the stern to work the large oar and I sat just in front of him. 'So you didn't die in the winter after all. I'm glad.' He looked intently at the way ahead and said nothing.

The sampan threaded its way southwards through a maze of narrow canals and then lurched and swayed as it entered a wider waterway. Some big junks with their sails rolled up, and a line of salt barges were moored on the far bank. We were in the Grand Canal. I remembered Cheng saying there were pirates in these parts, so I kept a careful look-out, feeling pleased at being able to do something to help.

We did not remain long in the Grand Canal, but soon turned into a tributary canal which flowed eastwards towards the sea. Before us a crimson sun had risen and streaks of red spread across the sky. The canal narrowed and became a small creek, just wide enough for one boat to pass. Apart from one or two solitary willow trees and the remains of broken old dykes, all that we could see was flat marshland. Southwards, through these marshes, lay the secret way to the hide-out of the ancient heroes. It was easy to see why the Mongol emperor's troops could not pursue them; all around us were pools of water bordered with reeds.

We had been travelling for a long time, but Cheng seemed tireless. The creek began to broaden and the water eddied and swirled against the sampan, when, around a bend, we saw the yellow waters of the Sea River above Taku. We turned into the river. On the eastern horizon lay a vast stretch of mud and there, looming over the estuary as if still commanding it, stood the last of the ancient Taku forts, a dark and brooding ruin.

'Y Jieh says the sea will disappear one day. The desert will swallow it up,' I said to Cheng. He made no reply, but turned the sampan around for our journey home. As he did so, I noticed a woman in blue working clothes standing among some rushes on the river bank. 'Y Jieh,' I called. The woman turned and looked at me. She was still standing there when we turned into the creek and she was lost to sight.

VIII

One summer's afternoon when there was not a breath of wind, I saw the stray-dog van from the police station being driven up and down the road by the wasteland. Sung Ge-Ge told me that the police were looking for some rabid dogs which were running wild about the Concession. That night it was too hot to sleep.

The pedlars did not come to our corner the next day, and I felt that an unknown danger was drawing steadily closer. In the evening long streaks of purple appeared on the eastern horizon. Then, with no warning, the typhoon struck. It was impossible to stand up in the wind and lashing rain. The wind eased and the rain fell more heavily. Soon, Meadows Road was under a foot of water; it looked like a river.

For three days and three nights the storm continued. My mother tried to calm her nerves by playing the piano, but every now and then she would suddenly stop and cry out, 'If the Yellow River breaks its banks we'll all be drowned!' This old fear about the Yellow River always returned to her during the summer rains. Pat tried to reassure her, but it was no good, for Captain O'Riordan had warned her that the republican government had neglected to repair the dykes and there was no telling when the Yellow River would change its course again and sweep through Tientsin.

When at last the flood waters subsided, our road was covered with evil-smelling mud and garbage. One or two dead dogs lay in the gutters. The weather became very hot again and the smell worsened. The first few cases of cholera were reported; then more and more of them. Like a fire, the cholera spread until all Tientsin was inflamed by it. People were seen dying in the streets. My mother took us to the Pasteur Institute in the French

Concession to be inoculated. A long queue of Chinese was standing outside, but there was a separate entrance for foreigners and we did not have to wait long.

Slowly, Meadows Road returned to normal and the pedlars came back to our corner, all except the old flower pedlar. I asked the other pedlars about him, but none of them had seen him. Weeks passed and still he did not come. Perhaps he had been swept away and drowned in the flood, I thought. Or maybe he had died of cholera. Then a more hopeful thought came to me. His flowers might have been swamped by the flood. When fresh ones grew, I might wake up one morning and once again hear his magical cry under the window: '*Bai lian hua.*'

The summer grew hotter. At the beginning of July my baby sister Stephanie fell ill with meningitis and was taken away to the hospital. She died there, two days later. My mother wandered about the house, talking about my father as if it was he who had just died and not my sister. She would look at the photograph of his grave with the Celtic cross in Shanghai and, with tears in her eyes, she would reproach herself for not having gone to his funeral. 'Only Brother Faust was there,' she said, again and again.

I, too, thought of my father after my sister's death. Like all babies who had been baptized, she would have gone straight to heaven where she would be ranked very close to the angels, and her wishes would get my father off many more days in purgatory than ever our prayers could. I told my mother this in order to comfort her, but she only stared at me blankly as if she did not know me.

Just before my tenth birthday, my mother had a nervous breakdown and was taken away to the hospital. I went there that evening, but I was not allowed to see her. 'Leave it for another week,' the matron said. 'She mustn't be disturbed now.' Mad Mac came to our house the next day and spoke to Y Jieh. That was when it was decided that she would take me with her to Shanhaikwan.

□

The sea! At last, the sea! I could hardly breathe, it was so wonderful. The green Pacific Ocean was spread out before me, moving and yet still. From the shore a blaze of gold on the water stretched far out to the horizon under the early-morning sun.

Laughing with excitement, I kicked off my shoes and, hopping over a line of black seaweed, ran across the sand to the water's edge. A wave raced towards me and its foaming white surf washed over my feet, pulling me after it as it retreated. Then another wave and another.

It was the first time I had ever seen the sea. A miracle was happening, I thought, and I laughed again with joy, feeling I was part of the whole universe.

Y Jieh and I had reached Shanhaikwan very late the previous night. All day I had been at the train window watching the countryside unfold. I had never left Tientsin before, and everything fascinated me. In the flat country north of the Russian Park, we came to the gaoliang fields. The rows and rows of yellow-green stalks, standing over eight feet high, seemed to me like an army of giants marching on Tientsin to avenge the imperial standard-bearer.

Late in the afternoon we left the plain behind and climbed slowly up to hilly and wooded country. The panting engine whistled and slowed to a walking pace when it crossed the frail-looking bridges over rivers swollen with yellow flood water. When it became too dark to see out of the window, I went back to Y Jieh. She was talking to some people from Manchuria. They said that the war-lord Chang Tso Lin was going to stop all the trains soon and this was their last chance to travel home.

At each station, more passengers got on the train until it was packed tight. Twice our train was stopped by soldiers and there was angry shouting between them and the train guards. Luckily, we were allowed to go on.

It was nearly midnight when Y Jieh woke me to tell me we were in Shanhaikwan. The train was besieged by people trying to get on and we had to struggle to get down the steps onto the platform. Not far from the station was the small Chinese hostel where a friend of Y Jieh was the cook and where we were to stay for our week's holiday. Although I was tired, I felt too excited to sleep. Early in the morning I heard the sound of the sea. It was a mysterious sound, gentle and strong at the same time. I tiptoed out of the room so as not to waken Y Jieh and ran down to the shore.

Now the sea I had so often dreamed about had come to life and I was wading in it. I splashed through some pools of shallow water to a long line of rocks and clambered onto them. I must be standing on the Manchurian border, I thought. Shanhaikwan meant 'the pass between the mountains and the sea'. Through this pass, in 1644, Manchu cavalry had swept into China with their banners flying, and the last Ming emperor had hanged himself from a tree in a garden of the Forbidden Palace in Peking. The soldiers of the Manchurian war-lord, Chang Tso Lin, were coming in daily by train through the same pass to fight Wu Pei Fu, and during the last week, many shops in Tientsin had closed their doors. But none of this troubled me at all. I felt that life was just beginning.

After looking out to sea for a long time, I turned to face inland. The line of rocks climbed up and became part of a big wall. Square-shaped forts rose up from the wall at intervals. Higher and higher the wall and its forts climbed up into the blue mountains until it disappeared over the top of them. It was the Great Wall of China. Once it had come down to the rocks where I was standing, but the sea had battered it down and now the Great Wall ended about a quarter of a mile from the shore.

Every morning, as soon as I got up, I came to this place on the rocks. On the fourth day, an old man leading a small brown donkey came along the beach towards me. He was bare to the waist and his blue trousers were full of patches. A large cone-shaped straw hat covered his head. When he reached the rocks, he looked up at me and grinned, showing two teeth.

'Would you like to ride the donkey?' he asked.

'Can I take your donkey up to the mountains?'

He turned to look at where I was pointing, then he leaned on the cloth saddle and laughed. I jumped down onto the sand and went up to the donkey to pat its neck. I had a feeling I was being drawn into what was happening, just as I had felt when the waves of the sea had tried to tug me after them. At the same time I felt free and brave enough for any adventure. The old man turned his head and I could see that he had a lump the size of an egg by his left ear.

'I have no money,' I said.

He shrugged. 'I am always here in the morning. I work in the gaoliang fields over there. Where will you go?'

'I would like to reach the top of the mountain where the wall crosses it, and see over the other side.'

He laughed again. 'What you see is not the top. If you were to reach the top it would be dark long before you got there. But you can go as far as the temple. It is a mile away. Keep to the top of the wall and you will see the temple among some trees below you.'

'Is it a Buddhist temple?'

'Buddhist!' The old man laughed. 'No, not up here in the north. It is dedicated to Confucius. But a little higher up, on the Manchurian side of the wall, you may visit the Shrine of the Rock if you have time. We farmers call it our temple.'

I got up on the donkey. The cloth saddle smelled strongly of garlic and sweat, just like the hunchback's bedding. 'Remember, keep to the top of the wall and you won't lose your way. I will see you coming down.' He gave the donkey a hefty smack and off it trotted, carrying me on my adventure. The donkey knew the way, for without any coaxing from me, it skirted the gaoliang field, crossed the railway tracks and made for the wall which loomed ahead. It was when we were crossing the railway lines that I first gave a thought to Y Jieh. I didn't think she would worry about me. Besides, it was too late to stop now. Feeling recklessly brave, I rode on.

At the foot of the wall, which was about thirty feet high, we followed a path until we came to a fort. A Union Jack was flying on top of it. In a field nearby were rows of white tents. This was the summer camp for British soldiers from Tientsin. A little way past the fort, our path sloped upwards and led us to the top of the wall, fifteen feet wide with a parapet on either side. Along this paved road on the wall's top, the imperial cavalry and war chariots used to race to any part of the wall that was threatened by invaders.

After about a quarter of a mile, I reached a second fort where the Italian flag was flying. Some Japanese soldiers on patrol were talking and laughing with an Italian sentry whose rifle was slung over his shoulder. They took no notice of me and I passed through an archway on one side of the fort. From now on the wall rose more steeply. It was broken in one or two places and my donkey had to pick its way down on loose blocks of stone before climbing again. In the fields below were masses of wild lilies and hydrangeas and lakes of blue irises. At one of the breaks in the wall we passed close to an orchard. There was not a soul about and I helped myself to a couple of pears.

I was now well up in the foothills of the mountain. The sun was hot and my donkey was sweating, so I halted for a rest in the shade of a ruined fort. Below me, the vast sea made the shore and the cluster of small houses by the railway look misty and fragile. I started to eat a pear and then, remembering the donkey, I gave him the other one. He dropped it to the ground and nosed it suspiciously before nibbling at it.

Ahead, the wall climbed up and up as if it was part of the mountains. From Shanhaikwan to the frontier with Tibet, this giant wall, which crossed mountain ranges and desert plateaux, had guarded China from marauding armies ever since it had been built two thousand years before. Y Jieh said there were many songs about the wall. Some of them mourned the people who had died building it. Apart from prisoners, masses of people had been rounded up by the emperor's soldiers and pressed into work on the wall. Blinded by the spring sand storms and frozen by the cruel winter winds, countless numbers of them had perished. Those who died were buried in the foundations of the wall, and there were stories that told of the sick being buried alive in this long stone tomb.

Few invaders had succeeded in penetrating the wall, but one enemy had conquered large sections of it. In the desert regions of the western Interior, the old wall had been covered by advancing sand dunes and only the tops of a few isolated forts stood out as a reminder of the once proud barrier. New sections of the wall had been built in modern times and the part near Peking had been restored, but many hundreds of miles of the original wall were slowly perishing each day under the relentless advance of the desert.

The hot crowded streets of Tientsin seemed very far away. Another cholera epidemic had broken out before I left, and the soldiers of two war-lords were menacing the railway station. Patrols of soldiers and police would be guarding the Concession's boundaries while the stray-dog van drove about the streets, hunting down its snarling and yelping prey. I hoped my mother was better. Summer was always a bad time for her. Perhaps the matron at the hospital would let me see her when I got back.

These thoughts of Tientsin disturbed me and dampened the excitement of my adventure. Looking up at the towering mountain I felt very lonely and wondered if I should go back. Then I thought of the cheerful old peasant who had let me have his donkey. The sight of it nibbling away at the pear made me laugh and the whole joy of the adventure came back to me. I mounted the donkey, gave its ribs a light tap with my heels and on we went, clattering along the high stone road.

At the next fort I saw a grove of pine trees on a hillock below the wall. Through the branches, yellow tiled roof-tops glinted in the sun. I came down from the wall and soon found a path which wound up the hillock through an avenue of trees. At the end of the avenue there stood a high, open ceremonial gate with pillars and across the top a blue scroll with Chinese characters painted on it. Through the gate I could see a white marble bridge.

My donkey ambled through the gate as if it had been to this place many times. Ahead of me the bridge spanned a pool full of red and white water-lilies. Just inside the gateway a group of Chinese were sitting in the shade of a big tree. Several ponies were tethered to a rail beside them. I got off the donkey and led it towards the men. One of them called out something to me and pointed to my donkey. Its mouth was dripping with saliva. It must have been the pear, I thought. Some of the pony men laughed and jeered, but they stopped when they saw a monk in black robes crossing the bridge with a party of foreigners. They were smartly dressed and had cameras slung round their necks. A woman member of the party ran ahead of the others and called out, 'One last snap, everybody! Look happy.' Then she knelt to photograph the smiling group on the bridge. One of the men, who was smoking a cigar, took something out of his wallet and handed it to the monk who bowed and tucked it up his sleeve. There was a lot of laughter as the visitors mounted their ponies and trotted away with the pony men running behind them.

The monk turned to me. 'You have come from Shanhaikwan? Where do you live?'

'Tientsin. My father came to Tientsin from Ireland. I was born in Tientsin.'

'Ah, the Ford of Heaven. Fords and bridges are important in life. That is why in China we build our bridges with the most beautiful stone. But the Ford of Heaven, that is the most important crossing of all.' He beamed with pleasure, and a vague memory came back to me of Brother Superior smiling at his own words when he made a witty speech.

'Did this place belong to the Emperor of China?' I asked.

'You refer to the yellow tiles? It is true that the great Ming Emperor, Yong Lo, deigned to give us his patronage. His name is on the gateway. You speak Chinese very well. Can you also read Chinese characters?'

'We are not taught Chinese at school, but Jieh-jieh, my amah's daughter, has taught me some.'

'It is good to study the characters. Language is the soul of a people. Come, I will show you the temple. You may leave your donkey there.'

I tethered my donkey. It had recovered and was drinking from the trough under the rail.

I followed the monk across the bridge and into a courtyard surrounded on three sides by low buildings. Facing us, at the top of a flight of steps, stood the dark red pillars of the temple entrance. Above the curved, yellow-tiled eaves I could see pine trees and the jagged mountain tops.

'Once there were a hundred monks and scholars here,' the monk said as we crossed the courtyard towards the temple. 'We had an excellent library, and people in Peking, Tientsin and some of the Manchurian cities sent their children to study here. Now we are only six and it is all we can do to keep some of our buildings in repair.'

We walked up the steps. 'Do the war-lords' soldiers ever attack you here?' I asked him.

He smiled. 'Soldiers are too lazy to climb up here. Nowadays they travel and fight in railway trains.'

It was dark inside the temple. Two red lanterns with long tassels hung down from the ceiling on either side of a black lacquered table on which incense was burning. The smoke curled up towards the statue of a bearded man standing behind the table. He wore the tall square-shaped hat of a scholar. The monk bowed to the statue. 'The Master, Confucius,' he said.

There was a long silence. Confucius' lips were curled in a faint smile. His eyes gazed serenely ahead of him. As I became accustomed to the half light, I noticed a figure in black kneeling in the shadows beside the table.

'I presume you know,' said my guide, 'that Confucius lived not far from Tientsin, in Shantung Province. It is said that the Master came here once from Shantung. No doubt he passed through the Ford of Heaven on his way. Those tablets on the wall bear the names of seventy-two of his disciples. Can you read the characters above them? They are the Master's teaching: *Respect authority; practise filial piety; observe the rites; achieve harmony.*'

He bowed to the statue and moved away. At the door, I turned around for a last look. The bearded Master was still smiling, but I could no longer see the kneeling monk who was hidden in the shadows.

The light was blinding outside in the courtyard. The monk led me to a gnarled old mulberry tree in the corner. A lizard ran across the paving stones at my feet. Beside the tree was a well. The monk lifted its wooden cover and began to pull on a rope which hung down the well. After a long time, when the slimy green coils of rope had piled high on the ground, a bucket came up dripping with water. In it were bottles of Pilsner lager and lemonade.

'I have no money,' I said.

He smiled. 'You are at school. Study hard to become a good scholar. That is the best way to show gratitude for the good things in life.'

I chose a bottle of lemonade and, lifting the glass ball top, I drank greedily. It was deliciously cold. The monk smiled and went to an alcove by the tree. He returned with some dates and cold sweet rice wrapped in mulberry leaves. While I was eating, he lowered the bucket into the well and replaced the lid.

'You are returning to Shanhaikwan now?' he asked.

'No. I am going to the other temple. The man with the donkey called it the Shrine of the Rock.'

A frown came over his face and his eyes had the same hurt look as Brother Paul's when my mother had explained one day that I couldn't serve mass at the school chapel on the feast of Corpus Christi because Father Molinari wanted me to sing at Notre Dame. But he quickly recovered his composure. 'The other temple, as you call it, is really only a terrace of rock. Do not expect any shelter there. It is true that a Taoist hermit once used it as a shrine, but he went away a long time ago. Do you know anything about the Taoists? Some of their writings are very beautiful.'

'Y Jieh, our amah, says the Tao means the way of nature.'

'Ah, yes,' he said, and the troubled look returned to his face. 'They are always wandering about, those Taoists, never still, always upsetting things. Nature is like that sometimes, it is true.'

We walked over the bridge to the gate and I untied my donkey. 'It is not always safe to go there,' he said. 'It is on the Manchurian side of the wall, although not far. Go back to the wall. A little higher up, it is broken. Descend there and you will see on the hillside above you a wall of rock. There is a rough path up to the left of it.'

At the gate the monk bowed and said, 'Honour and obey your parents. I wish you peace.' He sounded just like Father Molinari at the end of confession. Perched on my donkey, I waved to him as he stood in the gateway, smiling his thin sad smile.

When I reached the top of the wall the donkey wanted to go back downhill to Shanhaikwan, and I had to pull hard on one rein and dig him in the ribs to make him climb. Only a hundred yards on, the wall was broken and we came down to the Manchurian side. A herd of white-spotted deer stood motionless, looking at me; then they glided up the mountain-side and disappeared behind a wall of light red rock. I followed them until I reached the foot of the rock which was about six feet high. I got off my donkey and led him up the left-hand side to a natural terrace no more than fifteen yards long and five yards wide.

Long grass and one or two stunted old trees grew up between slabs of rock on the ground. I could hear water falling from a stream above. I tied the donkey to a tree and walked to the edge of the terrace. Below, the Great Wall snaked its way downhill, hidden now and then behind shoulders of land. The sea was now a dark blue.

There was no sound save for the falling stream. Standing there, I felt wonderfully free. Free to imagine and think whatever I wished, without anyone to stop me. After a while, I turned to face the mountain. It was then that I noticed, at the far side of the terrace, a slab of rock which was more upright than the others. I walked towards it. When I was about a yard away, I heard a rustling noise and thought I must have disturbed a lizard. I went round to the far side of the rock, but I could see nothing in the long grass. As I raised my eyes, I saw some Chinese characters, two inches high, carved in the side of the rock. There were ten of them in two vertical columns. Some were worn and faded; of the others, I knew only three – Sea, King and River.

The east wind had freshened and was making the grass bend. I looked up the mountain-side hoping to catch a glimpse of the deer again, for they had looked so mysterious and beautiful, but they had vanished. After the temple with its walls and pillars and its tiled roofs, this place was as empty as the tabernacle at Notre Dame on Good Friday when the altar was stripped bare, the small curtains over the tabernacle were drawn back and its door was left wide open to show that Christ was no longer there. Perhaps all empty ruins which were open to the sky and through which the wind could blow, had a special mystery, I thought.

A large bird of prey, dark in colour, hovered in the sky above and then wheeled and glided away so swiftly that in a few seconds it was only a speck in the distance. It might have been an eagle. How quickly wild creatures like the eagle and the deer came into sight and then were gone, leaving the rocks they touched so lightly to remain unchanged for centuries. I, too, had been in this place for only a few minutes and I would never come back here again.

Looking out to sea, I whispered a farewell prayer to the wind. 'Help me to be content to pass by even the most beautiful places without wanting to remain in them for long or to keep them for myself.'

On the way down, I thought of the characters on the rock. Sea, King, River. What did they mean? Was there a sea king?

In Shanhaikwan the sound of people talking in the streets was a shock after the silence of the mountain. I realized with a pang of sorrow that the strange sensation of lightness and spontaneity I had felt at the Shrine of the Rock had left me.

The next day, Y Jieh and I went to look for the book pedlar who toured the streets near the station. We found him squatting on the ground, drinking a bowl of tea. I told him about the characters carved in the rock, and asked him what they meant. He laughed and put down his bowl. 'You have been to the Shrine of the Rock,' he said. 'Your characters are from an old

Taoist saying.' He took a sheet of paper and a brush and ink stone from one of his baskets. Kneeling down, he mixed some ink with water, dipped his brush in it and rapidly drew two lines of characters which he read out to us:

'How did the sea become king of the many rivers and streams?'

'Through being lower than they.'

□

The train for Tientsin steamed into Shanhaikwan from Manchuria. This time it was not at all full. Most of the passengers were soldiers. We found seats as far away from them as possible. Y Jieh hated soldiers. They were worse than locusts, she said. When they went to villages far from their homes, they looted everything they could find. Only the worst people became soldiers and there was an old saying about them among the Chinese. 'One does not use good iron to make nails.'

With a long blast from its whistle, the train began to move. It was sad not to be able to see the sea from the carriage window. I thought of the different colours and the waves as well as the calm of the miraculous, ever-changing ocean. Remembering my view of the sea from the mountain-side, I crossed to the other side of the carriage and caught a last glimpse of the Great Wall high up in the mountain tops before they faded, together, into a distant blue.

At Chang Li, three stops after Shanhaikwan, the train was besieged by fruit sellers and Y Jieh bought a basket of apples. Another blast on the whistle and we moved on again. We began to descend now, leaving the hills behind as we entered the north China plain and chugged along towards the Ford of Heaven.

10 Victoria Road, Tientsin, showing Gordon Hall (left) and the Astor House Hotel.

11 D'Arc's Hotel in Racecourse Road during the flood of 1926.

12 Brother Paul with acolytes of St Louis College. Pat is fifth from the left, Brian
on the far right.

13 The chapel of the Jesuit college.

14, 15   Patrick (left) and Brian Power in 1935.

16   Staff and pupils of the British school. 1935. Brian is seated on the right.

17   In the foothills of the mountains, under the Great Wall.

18   The Great Wall near Shanhaikwan.

PART TWO

The Turn of the Tide

潮
流
在
轉

IX

'Welcome the Argyll and Sutherland Highlanders!' Through the paper arch by Gordon Hall, the Scottish regiment marched, answering the blazing crackers with the shrill sound of bagpipes.

It was a proud day for the chairman of the British Municipal Council, Mr Peebles, who took the salute. His guest of honour, the young ex-emperor Pu Yi, clapped his hands in delight at the pipers dressed in their green-and-black tartan.

Everyone in the Concession was relieved to know that the British garrison had been doubled. Recently, fired by nationalist fervour, a Chinese mob had stormed the British Concession in Hankow and destroyed the British war memorial and the Customs building. Within a month the Municipal Council there had been dissolved and the Concession had been meekly handed over to the Chinese republican government, now known as the Nationalists. What was to prevent the same thing happening in Tientsin? 'The principle of extra-territoriality is at stake,' Woodhead declared in his leader. That principle, enshrined in the Treaty of Tientsin, gave the foreign powers the right to administer their Concessions without interference from the Chinese, he reminded his readers. They must stand up to the Nationalists.

The virtual dictator of the Nationalists was General Chiang Kai Shek. He approved of the American 'Open Door' policy for trade in China, but he was against the foreign Concessions which he saw as an affront to Chinese pride. With the moral and financial support of America and a powerful army under his command, he had marched northwards and seized control of Peking.

The atmosphere in Tientsin became tense. Some Nationalist

troops tried to parade through the streets of the Japanese Concession, and were stopped by Japanese soldiers. My mother, who had recently come back from hospital, was frightened. Captain O'Riordan came to the rescue. 'In my opinion,' he said, 'the Scottish soldiers are the finest fighting men in the world. We couldn't be better defended.'

Scots or no Scots, people worried that a mob might one day rush into the Concession as it had done in Hankow. During those anxious times, the foreign residents of Tientsin were like the settlers in the Wild West films who waited behind their stockade for the next Red Indian attack. Smoke signals had been seen in the hills.

When, finally, the attack came, it was from a grim and silent enemy. For nearly a year there had been no rain in north-eastern China. In the summer of 1929 the Sea River was reduced to a trickle of water and only sampans could move in its muddy channel. One night the locusts thudded against our windows again. They were the first terrible warning of the famine that was to bring death to millions in the northern plain.

Appeals for help went out to the world. An international Famine Relief Commission sent supplies of food by ship to Tientsin, but that was as far as most of it got. The war-lords commanding the districts around Tientsin would not let any trains through to the famine-stricken areas in case they were kept there by their rivals. So, while the godowns along the bund were filled with food, the peasants in the surrounding country-side starved.

One day we saw a giant plume of black smoke rising across the river. Word soon spread that the Standard Oil Company's storage tanks were on fire. The fire service, police and troops were rushed to the scene, a new industrial area near the Russian Park. Only a few of them could take the ferry. The fire engines and the soldiers had to go by the long route, crossing the Austrian bridge. When they reached the fire it was out of control.

The Watch Committee suspected arson. Every available soldier and policeman was used to comb the riverfront for the saboteurs. HMS *Hollyhock*, accompanied by two police launches, sailed down river to search any suspicious-looking sampans.

While all this was happening, a long line of carts drawn by mules arrived at the entrance of the old imperial granary by the market-place. A solitary policeman on duty watched as the gates were opened from the inside. The carts trundled into the yard where a gang of coolies began loading them with sacks of rice and millet. As soon as each cart was loaded, it made off for the terminus of the Grand Canal where a fleet of barges was waiting.

This daring operation gave the society of the White Lotus the biggest haul it had ever made.

For three days the cloud of black smoke hung over Tientsin. Then it slowly drifted away, leaving its dark ashes on our window-sills and on the naked branches of the umbrella tree.

□

I was with my mother in the front garden one day when we heard the sound of a brass band coming from the direction of the wasteland. You could tell it was a Chinese band for it was all out of tune. My mother was the first to recognize what they were playing: 'It's a Long Way to Tipperary'. 'Of course!' she said. 'It's General Liu Ching Li's funeral today.' Two weeks after the big fire, the good war-lord had been found dead in his railway coach outside Tientsin station.

We went upstairs to get a better view. Two paper giants, one white and the other black, swayed at the head of the funeral procession. Each giant wore cardboard armour and brandished a sword. About twenty feet tall, they were supported by wooden frames which were carried by teams of coolies. Other coolies held guide ropes to steady the giants in the wind. A steward walked along the pavement, shouting orders at the coolies.

As the giants drew level with our house, the steward gave the signal to halt. The coolies lowered the giants to the road and sprawled on the ground. The giants' faces were only just below our window. The black one glared with angry eyes, while the white one smiled in triumph, his sharp teeth bared.

A crowd of Chinese began to gather, lining both sides of the road. With their trombones in front still blaring away, the brass band stumbled to a halt behind the giants.

> 'It's a long, long way to Tipperary,
> But my heart lies there.'

The bandmaster waved his stick and the music stopped. Some of the bandsmen took off their plumed helmets and unbuttoned their Prussian-style tunics to squat beside their instruments, while others crowded round the tea pedlar on the corner who was serving bowls of tea as fast as he could.

The procession moved off again. Twelve horsemen, dressed in the ancient uniform of the Tartars, came by, mounted on Mongolian ponies. Behind them marched long columns of soldiers followed by detachments of police from the foreign Concessions. First the British in their smart khaki uniforms and black polished boots, then the French, Belgians, Italians and Japanese.

After the police had gone by, the procession halted again and we went downstairs for something to eat. When I returned to the window, lines of Buddhist monks were passing. Each group was led by a row of monks tinkling little bells and chanting while the rest told their beads. Some of them were young boys. Their heads were shaven and they looked pale and thin. I wondered if they were acolytes. The Buddhists believed some strange things. One of their sects taught that nothing in the world was real. There was an old story about them which I had never been able to understand. One day, the story went, two monks were looking at a flag waving in the wind. Was it being moved by the wind? Or was it moving by itself? They could not agree. A Buddhist patriarch settled the question for them. 'The only movement that is real,' he said, 'is within your own minds.'

The procession had been passing for about two hours when I heard a low booming noise. Then the Lamas from Tibet appeared. They wore saffron robes and big hats with tassels hanging from them just like the cardinals' hats in the picture of heaven at school. Behind the Lamas six coolies carried a huge horn decorated with yellow tassels. Now and again a Lama blew on the horn. Its sound, deep as a fog-horn, echoed through the street and made our windows rattle. At this awesome noise, some small children in the crowd became frightened and cried.

The personal servants and retainers of the dead war-lord walked behind the Lamas, carrying trays piled high with token money made of silver paper. This was intended for the expenses Liu Ching Li would have to meet on his arrival in heaven. There was a bustle of excitement in the crowd. The coffin was coming at last! Draped in a white pall, it rested on top of a high wooden scaffolding carried by a hundred coolies. Behind the coffin, teams of coolies carried the sedan chairs of the women mourners; first the widow, then the concubines. The curtains on the windows of the sedan chairs were all drawn so that no one could see inside them, but at one of the windows I noticed a pale hand lifting a corner of a curtain and a white-powdered face peering out at the crowd lining the street.

Slowly, the black and white giants, the soldiers and the monks led the war-lord's coffin across Tientsin. Long after the tail of the procession had disappeared I could still hear the solemn sound of the Lamas' horn and in between its deep reverberating booms, sounding fainter and fainter, the jaunty march of 'It's a Long Way to Tipperary'.

□

Early in 1930 an announcement appeared in the *Peking and Tientsin Times* which left its readers stunned. The editor in chief, H.G.W. Woodhead, CBE, had resigned. He was leaving for Shanghai to edit the quarterly journal *Oriental Affairs*.

Tributes to Woodhead of a kind that are usually reserved for obituaries, poured in to his old paper. People of many nationalities as well as leading Chinese businessmen agreed that his was the voice of authority in Tientsin. They remembered with awe his frequent pronouncement that 'Britain should have conquered China rather than India.' If she had, Woodhead used to say, there would have been no limits to China's prosperity. China would have enjoyed an efficient police force, well-organized motor transport, uniform taxation, a balanced budget and, above all, a legal system second to none.

In the end, though, it was for his defence of the motor-car that many people would remember Woodhead. In the past year or so, the number of cars on the roads had increased so rapidly that traffic policemen had to be placed at the main crossroads in the Concession. To the mule-drivers, rickshaw coolies and bicyclists, who were all used to meandering freely, the motor-car was a menace. There were many angry scenes between them and the car drivers. Pat and I were in Taku Road one day when we saw a crowd surrounding a car which had collided with a rickshaw.

People were jeering at the driver, an Italian. Some coolies from one of the godowns came running up and together with the rickshaw coolie, they lifted the car and turned it over on its side. At the same time, riots were reported in Peking after a motor-car had knocked down and killed a rickshaw coolie there.

Woodhead spoke up for the car driver. In every fatal motor-car accident, he said, the mere fact that death had been caused was seen by the Chinese as the fault of the car driver. For primitive men such a view had been quite natural. Indeed it had been the orthodox view in Biblical days. 'In these enlightened times, however, when China is supposed to have assimilated Western principles, such reasoning can only be looked upon as archaic.'

Foreigners as well as Chinese suffered from Woodhead's strong words. A fearless exposer of injustices, the Old China Hand upset many foreign traders by his articles denouncing the export of coolies from Chinese ports and the conditions of slavery under which small children worked in some Tientsin factories.

Evidence of Woodhead's influence could be seen and felt all over Tientsin. Was it not his demand for action that had led to the setting-up of the Watch Committee? And was it not his constant pressure on the United States' government in article after article, that had brought the American Marines here and increased the number of American troops to over two thousand? When Woodhead spoke Washington trembled.

The title of Most Favoured Nation, granted to Britain by a Manchu emperor, had not been won lightly, Woodhead declared. But the American 'Open Door' policy would do away with it overnight. With characteristic bluntness, he accused the Americans in China of being parasites and hypocrites. 'The USA is a hermit crab that takes up its abode in the shell of another,' he charged. 'Tientsin was opened up by British arms and a British treaty. American businessmen and missionaries thrive here, yet they boast of their righteousness in having no territorial concession. Worst of all, American pacifist missionaries are engaged in anti-British agitation.' By the time Woodhead's outbursts reached England, Whitehall, too, must have trembled.

The Tientsin Club, of which Woodhead was a founder

member, gave him a splendid farewell dinner. All the foreign consuls and senior military officers attended to pay their respects to this mandarin of journalists. As his old newspaper put it, his going signalled the end of an era in Tientsin.

□

The slimy creek hardly moved. It was almost high tide and only a foot or so of mud and sludge was left on the bank above the water level. I was looking down from the grey stone bridge where the creek disappeared underground.

Plop! One or two bubbles rose in the middle of the water near some melon peel and cabbage leaves floating on the surface. It must have been a dogfish, I thought. This was where Pat and I had come fishing the first time I had played truant from school. We sat on the bank under the bridge where we couldn't be seen and Pat caught a small dogfish. The tips of my fingers burned as I recalled how the next day Brother Superior had caned me on each hand.

A fat toad hopped in the mud and then, as if too heavy to move any further, squatted by the still water's edge.

In the pale blue afternoon sky I could just see the faint circle of the full moon looking like a transparent wafer. It seemed so frail it gave you the feeling that the moon had spent itself and no longer had the magical force to make the seas rise and fall.

I gazed down at the creek again. The stagnant water looked, deceptively, as if it would remain at high tide always, like a proud invader who had come to stay. Then, gradually, some garbage floating not far from the toad began to turn and I knew that under the surface the water was not really motionless. Hard as it was to imagine, this evil-smelling creek was linked with the sea and through it, with all the oceans and waters of the world. In a strange and mysterious way the Sea River seeped in here beneath this bridge. Then slowly, very slowly, its waters would recede again until by evening the toad would be left high on the black mud and its deposit of refuse.

I had come to say goodbye to the old creek, for the next day we were moving to a house in the southern part of the Concession. Now that it was time to go, I felt sad. Would I find the creek much changed when I returned here? There was talk of covering more of it over, doing away with the bridge and building houses on the wasteland.

Tientsin had changed so quickly in the last year or two, I thought as I wandered slowly homewards. Many more foreigners had come to live in the Concessions. Mostly business people, they were much better off than the Siberian refugees of the old days. On New Year's Day, 1930, because he had heard that Grandfather d'Arc had left us some money, the butcher at the market sent us a plump turkey instead of the usual scrawny bustard. He also sent a foreign-style greetings card wishing us 'a happy and prosperous New Year'.

You only had to see the number of motor-cars and the new offices and shops in Victoria Road, to tell how prosperous people in the British Concession had become, as if those wishes exchanged at New Year really did come true.

The new buildings copied the 'classical' style of the Hong Kong and Shanghai Bank with its columns and its portico faced with marble. The biggest of them was the new head office of the Kailang Mining Administration. It looked like one of the huge temples the ancient Romans used to build in thanksgiving for a victory. I had seen one in an old silent film called *The Last Days of Pompeii*. It made an awesome spectacle as it crashed down in a sea of molten lava while Herr Schneider played furiously on his violin.

On the other side of the park, Gordon Hall, once the pride of the British Concession, now looked like a decaying monument. The Astor House Hotel, another relic of the past, seemed more like a drab saloon in a cowboy film than the grand hotel it had once been.

The new architecture spread like an invading army. One by one, the old buildings like the Tientsin Club surrendered to the new fashion. In Racecourse Road the Masonic Hall next to d'Arc's Hotel was given a 'classical' facade. It made my grandfather's old place appear like a forlorn but brave outpost besieged by alien buildings.

□

Four coolies loaded our furniture on to a big cart. Drawn by two mules, it trundled along Meadows Road in the direction of the

Grand Canal. It took four trips for everything to be moved. While the cart was being loaded for the last time, I went to say goodbye to the pedlars on the corner.

'Drink some tea,' the tea pedlar said. 'Any one you like.'

'Can I have the green one?'

He opened one of the little drawers, dropped a few dark green leaves into a bowl and filled it with boiling water. Leaning against the wall under the umbrella tree, I drank my favourite tea while the pedlar squatted beside his chest. 'You will like your new house,' he said. 'It is beside the Min Yuan sports field.'

The cart was about to move off. Y Jieh and Jieh-jieh were waiting for me at the gate. I finished my tea and handed the bowl to the pedlar. 'If you ever see the old flower pedlar again,' I asked him, 'will you tell him where we have gone?' He said nothing, but nodded his head and sighed as he put the bowl away.

Y Jieh, Jieh-jieh and I walked behind the cart. At one bridge where we had to cross a creek, the road was too steep for the mules and the coolies had to push the cart from behind. Soon after that bridge we turned left into Elgin Avenue. A quarter of a mile along it, we turned into Edinburgh Road. On one side was a row of new houses; on the other was the Min Yuan, a field with a cinder track running round it. Clumps of bushes and a few trees bordered the field.

The cart stopped outside the last house in the row. Sung Ge-ge was there to help the coolies. In the small front garden was a lilac tree and a few shrubs. My mother was delighted with the view from our drawing-room, which looked out onto the Min Yuan. The servants' quarters were exactly the same as those in our old house, with a backyard leading down to the basement. The part of the house I liked best was the flat roof garden.

When all our furniture had been put in place, the picture of St Patrick was hung on a landing at the top of the house. In the drawing-room St Patrick's place of honour was taken by a new picture. A copy of a painting by Constable, it showed a peaceful rural scene in England where oak trees shaded a thatched cottage and a friendly sheep-dog watched as cows grazed in a lush meadow.

A Russian groundsman named Nikitin worked in the Min Yuan. Pat soon made friends with him. He was a refugee from

Siberia where he had been a soldier. His pale blue eyes were usually bloodshot, and his straw-coloured hair and bushy beard looked as if they had never been brushed or cut. He wore a faded green smock over which he tied a piece of rope which served as a belt.

Nikitin and Pat would sit in the long grass at the edge of the running track smoking Chinese cigarettes and talking in Russian with such a strong Siberian accent that I couldn't understand what they were saying. Nikitin spent all his wages on cheap gaoliang wine which he kept in a beer bottle by his side. I never saw him eat anything. On his pay-day you would be sure to find him lying on his back in a drunken stupor, usually in the shade of a bush. Once a policeman found him lying on the pavement outside the Min Yuan and arrested him. A small crowd of Chinese watched as Nikitin was led away, muttering curses in Russian.

My mother settled down remarkably well in the new district, away from the old grey battlements at the centre of the Concession. When she played the charming music of Cheminade and gazed over the piano at Constable's pastoral scene, she seemed more at peace than I had ever known her. But it was too good to last.

One afternoon a letter came from Brother Superior announcing that Pat had been expelled. For a long time Pat had been a bad influence, the letter said. He had been punished time and time again for playing truant. Now he had done something which Brother Superior found hard to put into words. It was the most scandalous thing that had ever happened at St Louis. Brother Alphonse had been called away from his classroom. He returned unexpectedly early to find the place in an uproar. The boys were circulating something which Brother Alphonse confiscated. It was a grossly indecent cartoon of all the Brothers. Pat had admitted it was his work.

At school the next day, Kravchuk gave me the details. In Pat's cartoon the Brothers were all stark naked except for their white neck-bands. There was no mistaking each of their faces. They were sitting in the branches of a tree behaving like monkeys. Some were scratching themselves while others swung from branch to branch. Below the tree, Brother Superior rode on the back of an elephant as Tarzan used to at the pictures.

Her son expelled! My mother, who recovered very quickly from the shock of this news, was furious at the insult to our family honour. That night, the dark ominous rumblings and sudden sharp attacks of Chopin's 'Revolutionary Study' rang out from our house and startled the people passing by as my mother played with all her passion. War had been declared.

My mother's reaction took everyone by surprise, not least Brother Superior. She informed him that she was withdrawing me from his school and would send me with Pat to the British school. Never again would she play the organ and never again would her son Brian sing in the school chapel.

Brother Faust called at our house and did his best to placate my mother. 'Duty of a good Catholic parent. . . . Sin to send them to a Protestant school. . . . A co-educational one as well. . . . The bishop thinks. . . . Brother Superior might consider. . . .' But it was no use. Her mind was made up.

X

'A good school is the gateway to a successful life. Do you boys know who said that?' asked Captain O'Riordan.

'Confucius?' I ventured.

'Wrong again, my boy,' said the Captain, beaming with pleasure. 'Sir Francis Bacon.'

The Captain was elated at the news of our change of school. 'Now boys, mind you make the most of your new opportunities,' he went on, eyeing Pat as if to hint that it might be his last. Mrs O'Riordan smiled at us amiably and my mother poured out the tea. The Captain stood between us and the door. We were trapped. 'I have always taken the view,' he said, 'that life is a ladder to be climbed, and that each exam you pass, each qualification you obtain from your schooling takes you up a rung of the ladder. Isn't that so, Grace?' he asked, turning to my mother. She nodded and her eyes shone with gratitude for his paternal interest in us.

The British school had recently moved to a new building in Avon Road. The British ambassador had come down from Peking for the opening. There was a picture of him in the newspaper, sitting in the centre of a group of members of the Municipal Council and masters and mistresses in black gowns and mortar-boards.

The aims of the school, as stated in the prospectus, were to give its pupils a knowledge of 'the British way of life' and to prepare them for the University of Cambridge school certificate examinations.

Our school day began with assembly. At exactly five minutes to nine an electric bell rang and the whole school paraded in the spotlessly clean corridors. The smell of floor polish mingled with antiseptic reminded me of the Victoria Hospital. Between the two big hall doors hung portraits of King George V and Queen Mary of England. Under them was the school shield which bore a coronet in honour of Lord Elgin, crossed swords for General Gordon and a seahorse for Admiral Seymour.

At nine o'clock the bell rang again and Yang, the Number One Boy, wearing a Manchu gown, opened the hall doors. To a rousing chord on the piano played by Miss Ransom, the buxom art mistress, we marched into the hall and lined up facing the stage. Mr Hume, the headmaster, appeared from behind the heavy black curtains and stood at a lectern on the stage. After shuffling some papers, he took off his mortar-board and announced the hymn. His favourite one was 'There Is a Green Hill Far Away'. During it, he would take off his spectacles, dab at his eyes with his handkerchief and then hold it against his nose and mouth like a mask. I sometimes wondered if he might be thinking of a corner of England where he longed to be.

After prayers on my first day, Mr Hume read out his notices. Miss Ransom struck up the march 'The British Grenadiers' and we trooped out past the Number One Boy standing by the doorway like a war-lord taking the salute.

> 'But of all the world's great heroes
> There's none that can compare.
> With a Ta and a Ra, Ra, Ra, Ra,
> For the British Grenadiers!'

The brisk marching song was still ringing in my ears as I trooped into form IV with a file of boys and girls. Each pupil had his own desk and there was plenty of space between the rows. I found a vacant desk at the back and looked about me furtively. Potted plants were arranged along the window-sills and the walls were hung with pictures of English scenes: the Tower of London, Westminster Abbey and a thatched cottage in Stratford-upon-Avon. It seemed wrong to be in a schoolroom without pictures of hell, purgatory, heaven and limbo.

The children, about half the number there had been in Brother Paul's class, stood in groups chatting in an English which I understood only in snatches. When they giggled at their secret jokes I felt more of an alien than ever. The girls wore pretty coloured blouses and ribbons in their hair, and the boys in their clean shirts and ties looked much smarter than me. A mistress in a black gown came in and everyone stopped talking. Her name was Miss Wright and she taught English History.

I shrank into my seat and wished that I had magical powers so that I could make myself invisible. When I dared to look up, I saw that Miss Wright was chalking up on the blackboard, 'King James I of England, 1603–1625'. She underlined it and then turned round to look at us. Too late, I ducked. 'It's Brian Power, our new boy, isn't it?' she said. Everyone turned to examine me. I held on to my desk and then slowly levered myself up until I was half standing and half crouching.

'Yes, Miss.'

'Do you know any English history, Brian?'

'No, Miss.'

'Nothing at all?'

Two girls smiled at each other. I gripped the sides of the desk. 'Only a bit about the Irish famine and . . .'

'Yes?'

'And the Easter Rising.'

'I see. Well, this term we have reached the long and eventful reign of James the First.'

At last she stopped looking at me and I began to breathe more easily. 'It marks the beginning of modern England,' Miss Wright continued. 'A time of exploration and scientific thought when logic and common sense overcame old superstititions. Here are the important events.' She began to write on the board and everyone copied down her words in their notebooks:

> Gunpowder plot.
> King James Bible.
> Defeat of Catholic Spain.
> Work of Sir Francis Bacon. . . .

It was a bad morning for the Catholic Church.

□

There was no escaping Sir Francis Bacon. Whatever subject we happened to be studying, his name was sure to crop up.

Soon after the beginning of term a special celebration was held in the assembly hall to mark the opening of a science laboratory. The school's proudest possession, it had been donated by several Tientsin business firms.

The school governors sat in a row on the stage while Mr Hume addressed us in his solemn voice. Sir Francis Bacon, he said, was not only an eminent lawyer, statesman and orator, he was a leader of the reformation in scientific thought. None of us could fail to be inspired by his words: 'Man's sovereignty over nature is the grand object of all science . . . .'

As I listened to the headmaster's earnest speech, the feeling grew in me that Sir Francis Bacon was the nearest thing the British school had to a patron saint. But, as I was beginning to learn, the 'saints' of modern science took a very different road from the Taoist sages, the followers of the Way, who reminded us how small man is in the face of nature.

□

Mr Hardcastle, who was also the sports master, strode into form IV to teach us geography. A graduate of Manchester University, he was an expert on the Pennines, which he called 'the backbone of England'. The counties on either side of that range, Lancashire and Yorkshire, he told us, were the great cricket-playing counties. Especially Lancashire, he said with a smile, showing his white teeth. All the boys laughed. Mr Hardcastle seldom missed a chance to poke a little innocent fun at the headmaster, who was a supporter of Yorkshire.

My eyes wandered to a map hanging by the blackboard. What a different world it showed from the one I used to look at in Brother Paul's classroom! Now, the British Empire stood out in bright red, dominating the world, but the pale green of France and her colonies was hard to make out in the background. I would hear no more of St Louis the crusader. The chivalry of Catholic France, the Emperor Napoleon and General de Montauban were fast fading into a distant scene as if I had imagined it all. The common sense of Protestant England was now my real world, and King James, Sir Francis Bacon and the Pennine Range the objects of my study.

For all the many differences between St Louis College and the

British school, they had one thing in common. Neither the Marist Brothers in their white neck-bands nor the black-gowned masters and mistresses taught a single thing about China, its geography, its language or its history. But I would go on learning about China from the story-tellers in the market-place and from Y Jieh. Wise and strong as a rock that had been shaped by the weather, she put me in mind of the shrine above Shanhaikwan where only a mountain stream and the wind shared the deep silence.

□

Before we had been a month at the British school, Pat had introduced some of the boys to beedka. They played it in a secluded corner of the playground on the far side of a flight of steps which led up to the main entrance. The game caught on quickly and there was often a queue waiting to play. This annoyed the prefects, especially the senior prefect Peter Orloff, the son of Prince Orloff who lived in a large house in Romanoff Avenue. Peter was one of several White Russians at the school. Good-looking and talented, he had become more British than the British and was captain of athletics and football. He made it plain that he despised the newly imported Siberian game which disturbed the peace of the playground over which he ruled. From now on there was always a prefect to be seen hovering about on the top of the steps to keep an eye on the beedka game going on below. Within a short time, Pat was reported to the headmaster for gambling, smoking and using bad language.

The beedka exchange rate for cigarette cards had changed since our days at St Louis. Now, the cards of highest value were the Hollywood film stars, with sporting stars next, followed by uniforms of British army regiments. The cards of lowest value remained the Chinese landscapes and stories.

Pat still kept in touch with Kravchuk and Nakvasin from the old beedka gang at St Louis. They met regularly at the St Louis gate to exchange their duplicate cards. I hardly ever saw my old school friends. Once, when the playground at St Louis was full of boys swarming round the *piroshkee* man, I stood outside the gate watching them. I was wearing my smart British school blazer with the crossed swords of General Gordon on the breast pocket. I wanted to go in and find my friends, but I was afraid they would think me a deserter who had joined another army. I walked away feeling sad.

A little way down the road I came to the high wall of the warlord's palace. With a thrill of excitement, I remembered my promise to return one day to see the old eagle in its cage. I found the foothold and climbed up the wall to look down into the garden. There it was! Its curved beak and yellow eyes looked as fierce as ever.

□

One day a black motor-car drove up to the gates of the British school. A servant, who had been sitting next to the driver in front, got out and opened the car's rear door. A plump Chinese boy emerged carrying a brand-new satchel. He was dressed in a smart tweed jacket with shorts to match. He walked over to a group of us who had been watching his arrival, shook hands and, with a friendly grin on his face, announced that his name was James Ni.

James was the first Chinese boy to be admitted to the school. He was placed in my form and was given the desk in front of mine. He giggled a lot. At first I thought his giggling was a form of nervousness, but later I was not so sure. When Miss Wright left the room at the end of her lesson, James's shoulders would heave and he would break out into high-pitched laughter. I dreaded that she might hear him one day.

At four o'clock when school ended, the black motor-car would be waiting at the gates. James would wave goodbye to us from the back seat as he drove away down Avon Road.

One day James invited me to supper at his house. I was waiting by our front gate as the black car arrived. James's servant ushered me into the back seat. Luckily, nobody was watching. It was the first time that I had ever been in a motor-car. The chauffeur drove off and I sank back into the soft leather upholstery, trying to feel at ease. There was a thick carpet on the floor and, by my shoulder, a tube through which you could speak to the servant in front.

We drove into a long paved courtyard bordered with flowering shrubs in earthenware pots. When we stopped, the servant got out and opened the car door for me. He beckoned me to follow him into the house. The entrance hall was paved with plum-coloured tiles. A lantern with silk tassels hung down from the ceiling. On each side of the hall was a line of ebony benches. A scroll depicting an ancient battle ran along the walls. Horsemen, chariots and archers were marshalled for battle in a landscape of mountains while, on another section of the scroll, generals strode about conferring outside tented pavilions.

I had just reached the battle scene when James came running down the staircase at the end of the hall. 'Good, good, welcome,' he said. We went up the staircase to the main room on the first floor. I found myself in a different world. Downstairs everything had been oriental and austere; here was a foreign-style living-room. All the furniture was European. Framed photographs stood on the many cabinets and tables. A piano and a gramophone were on one side of the fireplace. On the other side was a large cabinet filled with objects carved in ivory.

On the wall above the fireplace hung the portrait of a general. His white uniform was decorated with gold epaulettes, rows of medals and a large star. His left hand rested on the hilt of his sword, while his right hand held a cap crowned by a blue plume. 'My father,' said James. 'He was what you call a war-lord. He captured three trains from Wu Pei Fu. Now he has retired.' James fell into an armchair and giggled. General Ni looked down at me sternly. 'Is your father at home?' I asked anxiously. James choked with laughter. 'No, no, no, he is on a visit to Japan.'

Japan! Without thinking, I asked, 'Does your father know Colonel Doihara?'

James looked at me sharply. His face was unusually serious. 'A clever man. They say he is going to catch one of the leaders of the Lotus society soon, a foreigner who travels between here and the Interior.'

Just then an old grey-haired servant appeared from behind a screen. His long black gown rustled as he walked over to James and announced that dinner was ready.

At dinner we had European-style food. The old servant filled our wine glasses with crème de menthe. One sip of the thick green liquid made my head whirl and my throat burn. James kept up a stream of jokes, but I hardly listened to him.

'A foreigner who travels between here and the Interior.' The words went on sounding inside my head. Could it be? I remembered thinking, 'You would make a perfect spy. . . .'

The sound of tinkling bells came from the courtyard below. Seeing me turn around, James stood up. 'Come and look,' he said, his face beaming. He flung open the windows and stepped on to a small balcony. A procession was coming towards us from a small house inside the main gate. A giant wearing a black skull-cap walked in front. He carried a wooden frame in the shape of a cross with small bells fixed to it. Now and again he shook the cross and the bells rang. Behind him, in pairs, walked twelve young girls dressed in bright pink gowns buttoned up to the neck. They seemed to be wearing white masks. As they drew nearer, shuffling along on their tiny bound feet, I saw that their faces were coated with white powder and that their cheeks had red spots painted on them.

James put his hand on my shoulder and chuckled. 'My father's concubines. They are going to their supper.'

'Why is the big man ringing the bells?'

'That's the eunuch. He is warning all our servants not to look at the girls. It is an old custom.'

The girls were almost under the balcony now. One of them looked up at me. Her face had the same blank expression as the concubine I had seen peering from the window of her sedan chair at the end of the funeral procession. I felt a deep pity for her and I hoped that James would not laugh. As if he could tell what I was thinking, he remained silent.

The last pair of girls disappeared from our sight and the sound of tinkling bells grew fainter and died away.

□

The late Queen Victoria's birthday, May 24, was also Empire Day. Woodhead used to say with pride that it was celebrated more heartily in Tientsin than anywhere in England.

The day began with a church parade. The Consul-General in his cocked hat attended the service at All Saints and afterwards reviewed the troops. HMS *Hollyhock*, dressed with flags, was open to the public.

In the afternoon the inter-schools sports meeting was held at the Min Yuan opposite our house. Mr Peebles was chief referee, assisted by the umpire, Captain 'Freezer' Frost, a short man with a large moustache waxed at the ends. After serving as a sergeant in the British Army in India, the Captain had found work as the secretary of the Tientsin Racecourse. He joined the Volunteer Corps and soon rose to his present rank.

Mr Peebles admired the Captain's efficiency. Wherever Mr Peebles presided as chairman, be it at the St Andrew's Society or the Ice Skating Club, you would be sure to find Captain 'Freezer' Frost, the perfect secretary, sitting by his side, armed with a battery of sharp pencils and plenty of paper.

Coloured penants fluttered around the Min Yuan and the cinder running track had been marked with white lines by Nikitin. Mr Hardcastle of the British school marched up and down, sporting an official's red, white and blue rosette in the buttonhole of his blazer. Captain Frost hoisted the Union Jack on a pole in front of the stand. It was the signal for the sports to begin.

After some junior events and an interval came the main event of the day, the relay race between the British school and St Louis College. The British school team were the favourites this year. They had a new star runner in David White, a tall, handsome Californian whose father was an officer in the American Marines. All the girls shrieked with delight when David White ran on to the track with Peter Orloff, the British school captain. Mr Hardcastle patted them both on the back and then walked to the finishing post to take up his position as one of the judges.

A small group of rough-looking boys from St Louis, some of whom were furtively smoking cigarettes, sat near the finishing post to watch Kravchuk lead their team out. Pat was among them and I hoped that Mr Hardcastle would not spot him for he was sure to think him disloyal. The swarthy Kravchuk, who looked more like an all-in wrestler than a runner, jogged up and down to loosen his bulging muscles. Years of hard work in the Siberian forests as a boy had made him very strong.

Captain 'Freezer' Frost fired his starting pistol and off went the first two runners. The British school quickly built up a lead and by the time Orloff started his leg, he was twenty yards ahead of Nakvasin. Then Nakvasin began to close the gap. When the last two runners seized their batons and raced off, Kravchuk was only a yard behind David White, and the girls in the stand began to scream. Ten yards from the finish, Kravchuk burst into the lead and won. There was loud cheering from the Siberian camp and Pat and his friends called out something in Russian to Kravchuk. It must have been funny for it made Kravchuk double up with laughter by the side of the track.

Mr Peebles presented the cup and medals to the winners and then made a speech. It was more important to compete than to win, he said.

Another Empire Day had come to an end. In the evening there would be a reception at the Tientsin Club followed by a banquet at the Astor House Hotel.

It was a balmy night and Pat and I pulled our mattresses on to the flat roof.

'I think Mr Hardcastle spotted you laughing with the Siberians,' I said. 'You'd better watch out. I'm afraid he's going to report you to the headmaster.'

Pat said nothing.

'What did you call out to Kravchuk at the end of the relay?'

'Oh, just before the race Captain Frost asked Kravchuk how old he was. The Captain and Mr Hardcastle think that Kravchuk is cheating about his age and that he is over the age limit for the school sports. So at the end we called out, "Old man Kravchuk." That's all.'

'Is he over-age?' I asked.

'Yes. But don't tell anyone,' said Pat.

More and more stars had come out and I could see the Milky Way. From somewhere in the Min Yuan came the sound of a man's voice singing. Nikitin! He sounded drunk and happy. What was he singing about, I wondered. A dark forest, perhaps, with snow on the ground between the tall fir trees. In the distance wolves howled while a boy ran along a path to warn the foresters that the Cossacks were coming.

XI

After we moved to our new house, we began to attend Sunday mass at the college of the Jesuit Fathers in Racecourse Road on the far side of the Min Yuan.

The Hautes Études Commerciales et Industrielles was an imposing red-brick building surrounded by iron railings. The central and most spacious part, which had windows reaching down to ground level, housed the famous science museum founded by Père Licent. Later, when the Jesuits opened their institute of higher studies for Chinese students, wings had been added to the museum. The chapel was at the far end of the south wing. Behind it, an avenue lined by ash trees led to the house where the priests lived. Beyond the priests' house, to the south-east, lay open country.

Brother Joseph, a native of Alsace Lorraine, was the lay brother in charge of the sacristy. He also had the task of keeping in touch with members of the public who used the chapel. He was a fat jovial man with a large wart on his nose and a straggly brown beard. In no time he enlisted our services. My mother agreed to play the organ and conduct the choir at the ten o'clock mass. I was to serve the eight o'clock mass as well as sing in the choir.

So Brother Paul lost an acolyte, and Father Molinari lost his organist and choir to the Jesuits. St Thérèse of Lisieux faded from our devotions and St Ignatius Loyola, the Spanish warrior who had founded the Society of Jesus to combat heresy, took the place of the Little Carmelite Flower.

'*Deus, qui ad majorem tui nominis gloriam propagandam.* . . . O God, who, for the greater glory of thy name, by means of blessed Ignatius didst reinforce thy Church Militant with a new army:

152

grant that by his aid we may so fight on earth as to be worthy to share his crown in heaven.' The thin sharp voice of the Father Superior finished singing the collect for the feast of St Ignatius and the deacon's procession formed up for the gospel. A cloud of incense rose up to the roof of the chapel. The deacon, a Chinese Father, cleared his throat and chanted the gospel in his careful Latin: '*Et dicebat illis; Messis quidem multa, operarii autem pauci.* . . . And he said to them; The harvest indeed is great, but the labourers are few. . . .'

For over three hundred years the Jesuits had fought to convert China to the Catholic faith. It had been the dream of St Francis Xavier who had died facing the inaccessible Chinese coast. Then came Father Matteo Ricci, whose heroic journey up the Grand Canal from the south had taken twenty years. Soon after Ricci's death in Peking, the last Empress of the Ming dynasty became a Catholic. That was to be the zenith of the Jesuits' achievement at the imperial court, for the Manchu barbarians then swept into China to usurp the throne.

'*Ite, ecce ego mitto vos sicut agnos inter lupos.* . . . Go, behold I send you as lambs among wolves. . . .' The gospel ended and the deacon gave the holy book to the celebrant to kiss.

From my very first visit to their chapel, I had been attracted to this order whose priests wore Chinese clothes and who were, nearly all of them, Chinese scholars. But it was on this feast of St Ignatius that I was captivated by the spirit of heroic adventure in the Jesuits as the mass reached its climax and the choir intoned the solemn words from St Luke: '*Ignem veni mittere in terram.* . . . I am come to send fire upon the earth; and what will I, but that it be enkindled?'

'*Ad majorem Dei gloriam*': A.M.D.G. was the motto of the Society of Jesus, and the Jesuits began their letters with it. I, too, started to put A.M.D.G. at the top of my written work at school. No one there had any idea what the letters meant, and writing them made me feel part of a secret society. Were the Jesuits not the arch spies and traitors of the English history books? I had joined the Counter Reformation!

□

The museum at the Jesuit college was open to the public on

Sunday afternoons, but I never saw more than a dozen people there. The large hall was a more silent place than the chapel itself. The Father Curator in his black gown moved discreetly about the exhibits, pausing now and again to whisper a word of explanation to a visitor.

Once when I was looking at a map of China on the wall, Father Curator appeared at my elbow and motioned me to follow him. He led me to a map in a glass frame.

'The earliest Chinese sea chart,' he said, 'made when the Chinese sailed their junks as far as the Persian Gulf and Africa. You can see China there at the centre of the world.'

'That's why the Chinese call their country *Zhong Guo*, the Middle Kingdom,' I exclaimed, and then blushed at my effrontery. Father Curator smiled forgivingly and glided away to another visitor.

Rows of glass cases stood in the middle of the hall. They were filled with fossils, bones and other traces of very early animals going back to the Stone Age. All that knowledge so tidily preserved and so painstakingly displayed in chronological order had a chilling effect on me.

Father Curator returned to my side. 'You must come and see the exhibition of photographs of the earliest man,' he said, guiding me to a room which led off the hall. '*Sinanthropus Pekinensis* is 500,000 years old, the missing link between ape and man. The scientists call him Peking Man for short. He is China's oldest and most valuable treasure.'

The pictures of the famous discoveries made in 1929 were arranged in a pyramid shape on one large wall. At the base were the fossils of sabre-toothed tigers and elephants which had lived in the forests. Above them were ostriches, water-buffaloes, deer and hyenas which had roamed the grasslands of north-western China in the time before the deserts began to spread so relentlessly. Higher still were some of the things which had been found in the ape-man's cave at Choukoutien, fifty miles south-west of Peking: the jaw-bone of an ape-man's child and some stone tools.

'Those black patches in the picture are ash and charcoal,' whispered Father Curator. 'Peking Man used fire not only to keep warm and to drive away wild beasts. He is the earliest being known to have used fire for cooking.'

Crowning all the other pictures was one of Peking Man's head, pieced together from fragments of bone and a few teeth. I moved away from Father Curator's side so that I could see for myself in silence. These bones had lain buried for centuries, had been dug up, classified, given a name, photographed and exhibited to our curious gaze. Was it just my imagination, or did this broken old skeleton look tormented? The warning of the Taoists came back to me. 'Do nothing against nature.'

□

On my way to the Jesuit college, I used to take a small path which wove between the shrubs bordering the Min Yuan. The entrance to it was hidden by a lilac bush. I hardly ever saw anyone on the path and I came to think of it as my own secret way. Sometimes I practised singing as I walked along it, and sometimes I would stop to watch a bird, but mostly I dreamed. I dreamed of Shanhaikwan and its sea and mountains, the deserts of the mysterious Interior, the marshlands to the south-east where the outlaws had their hiding place, and the coast of County Clare in the West of Ireland at the other end of the world.

When I reached the chapel, Brother Joseph would be waiting for me on the steps. If there was time, he would tell me something about the priest whose mass I was to serve. Even in the sacristy, where there was a rule of silence, I could tell from the mischievous twinkle in his eye or the way he lifted an eyebrow or tugged his beard, what Brother Joseph felt about the priest who was putting on his vestments.

The sacristy, which was behind the altar, was a long narrow room full of dark wooden cupboards where the priests' vestments were kept. A small window gave a view of the avenue of ash trees. On one wall, a figure of Christ carved from ivory hung on a black cross. This crucifix was a very old one and had been made by a Chinese lay brother. Under the crucifix was a prie-dieu where priests would kneel before and after they had said mass.

There were about twenty Jesuit priests at the college. Most of them were French, but there were also three Chinese and one Tibetan. Brother Joseph's favourite was the Tibetan, who had been a yak herdsman on the high plateau near Lhasa where his family had been converted by the Jesuit Fathers. That was in the time before the Lamas had closed their frontiers to all foreigners, and only the mountains had been an obstacle to travel in Tibet.

The Jesuits had been allowed to build a mission in Lhasa and for many years two of their priests lived with a handful of disciples in one of the clusters of small houses below the Potala palace. Over the thatched roof-tops fluttered hundreds of little coloured prayer flags which the Tibetans called 'horses of the wind'.

In the palace of the High Lamas, the Dalai Lama, like the Pope in the Vatican, was both spiritual and temporal ruler. Year after year, the Jesuit Fathers looked up over the streaming flags towards the palace on its table of rock, waiting in vain for an audience with the Most High One. Their mission ended when foreign warships and armies began invading China, and the Lamas decreed Tibet a forbidden land.

No foreigner was allowed to set foot there until 1904, when the British fought their bloody way up to Lhasa. When the soldiers entered the palace they found that the Dalai Lama had vanished. None could say where he had gone. Only one or two monks had seen a cart drawn by yaks leaving Lhasa in the night. It carried the Dalai Lama and a few followers through a little-known pass down the mountains into China where they were given refuge. The herdsman who had driven the Lamas' cart then took leave of his venerable master and made his way to Peking where he was received by the Jesuits.

'Maybe he is a Lama in disguise,' I said when I heard the Tibetan's story. Brother Joseph chuckled. From then on, to tease me, he always called our Tibetan priest 'the Lama'.

The first time I served the Lama's mass I arrived very early, feeling curious and nervous. A strong east wind was blowing, making the ash trees sway. Inside the sacristy Brother Joseph laid out the green vestments for the time after Pentecost and then placed a green veil over the silver chalice. I was putting on my surplice over my black cassock when the door opened, letting in a gust of wind. A thickset old man walked slowly but steadily into the sacristy. He stood before the vestments and sighed a long, deep sigh as if he was part of the dying wind. The back of his powerful neck bulged like that of an ox and his dark yellow head was bald except for a patch of white stubble behind his huge ears.

Dressed in his green robes, the Lama picked up the chalice and turned to face me. I stood there, petrified. His massive head, weathered by the sun and wind, looked as if it had been carved out of yellow-brown rock. High on his face, under his drooping eyelids, his cheekbones jutted out like two rock ledges. Brother Joseph coughed and I turned to lead the way into the chapel.

'*Introibo ad altare Dei.*' At the foot of the altar, the Lama recited the psalm in a continuous low-pitched drone like the deep noise made by the long Tibetan horn in the funeral procession. It was impossible to catch what he was saying. I searched in my mass book to find the place, but I could only guess. '*Mea culpa, mea culpa, mea maxima culpa.*' I was still striking my breast in the middle of the Confiteor, halfway through the psalm, when the Lama mounted the steps to the altar.

'*Gloria in excelsis Deo.*' Standing at the altar with his arms raised to shoulder level, he looked like a vast tree trunk. Strength and calmness radiated from him, and instead of my usual feeling of panic when I lost my place, I felt at ease.

The Lama intoned the gospel. Feeling confident now, I read it at my own pace. '*Considerate lilia agri. . . .* Consider the lilies of the field, how they grow; they labour not, neither do they spin. But I say to you that not even Solomon in all his glory was arrayed as one of these. . . . Be not anxious therefore. . . .'

By the time I had finished reading the gospel, the Lama had moved to the far side of the altar and was waiting patiently for me to offer him the wine and water for his chalice. At the lavabo he held out his brown hands while I poured water over his thick, scarred fingers. '*Lavabo inter innocentes manus mea. . . .* I will wash my hands among the innocent.'

I handed him a white linen towel. While he was drying his hands on it, a thought came to me. This old man from the high mountains of Tibet was part of raw, wild nature. That was what gave him his energy and his touching innocence. He walked in a world of silence, a world of rocks and trees. For the first time in my life I realized how beautiful was the silence of the mass.

'*Hoc est enim corpus meum. . . .* For this is my body.' Bowed before the altar, the Lama held the frail wafer of bread which had become Christ's body in his strong hands. In the stillness I found myself thinking of the Chinese character for 'contemplate' or 'study'. It was made up of two parts. On top was a roof, which symbolized a meeting; below was a human heart. Together they meant bringing a fact of the past into the heart at the present moment. The Lama ate the sacred host and past and present became one in him.

After his communion I poured water over his fingers into the chalice. '*Anima nostra, sicut passer. . . .* Our soul has been delivered as a sparrow out of the snare of the fowlers. The snare is broken and we are freed.'

'*Ite missa est.*' We left the altar and I walked ahead of the Lama into the sacristy. We bowed to the crucifix and to each other. After unrobing, the Lama did not kneel at the prie-dieu but left the sacristy immediately. On my way home, I saw his sturdy figure with head bent forward, walking up and down between the ash trees.

A swallow sliced through the air above the shrubs on my secret path. Watching it, I thought how miraculous the world was. The wildness of the birds, the green of the few trees on this path and the mysterious sacrifice of the Lama's mass when time had been one, moving and yet still like the sea at Shanhaikwan.

I was nearing the end of the path by the lilac tree when I noticed something on the ground. It was an empty bottle. Near it, in the gap between two shrubs, the grass had been pressed down. One or two cigarette-ends lay on the grass. Someone had been lying there. Then it came to me. Of course! Nikitin.

□

Two of the Jesuit Fathers came to tea at our house one day. Père Philippe, whom I knew, was short and fat with a bushy brown beard. He wore the traditional Chinese gown and skull-cap of the Jesuits in China. His arms flailed the air as he talked and laughed. The other Father was tall and thin. He wore a black clerical suit and white dog collar. On his head was a black felt hat with a high crown.

As they walked towards our garden gate, Pat, who had been standing there with me, disappeared. Père Philippe introduced me to his companion, but in the confusion I did not take in his name. His prominent nose was shaped like an eagle's beak; over it, a pair of very small eyes, set deep and close together, inspected me. Although he smiled, there was a melancholy air about him. I showed them into the drawing-room and went off in search of Pat.

'Père Philippe's friend was charming,' my mother said to me that evening. 'His name is Père Teilhard de Chardin and he comes from Picardy. I wish you had stayed because Père Teilhard talked about the hymn "Mon Dieu je ne suis pas digne" and how moved he was at hearing you sing it at mass. They used to sing it in his church in Picardy when he was a boy.' Her eyes filled with tears as she went on, 'Père Teilhard's sister was the superior at the convent of the Little Sisters of the Poor in Shanghai . . . where your father was taken . . . She died of smallpox there and is buried in the same cemetery as your father.'

Later that night Pat showed me a pen-and-ink drawing he had made of the two Fathers. Père Teilhard, who was riding a mule, wore his tall black hat and carried a lance. He was Don Quixote. Behind him, Père Philippe, as Sancho Panza, was riding a donkey and trying hard to keep up.

Brother Joseph told me that Père Teilhard de Chardin was the Father who had gone to Peking to work with the team of scientists after Peking Man had been discovered. When he was not away on expeditions, he worked in the museum with Father Curator.

Unlike the other Fathers at the college, Père Teilhard never wore Chinese clothes, and, what was stranger still, although he had been in China for many years, he spoke no Chinese. When I served his mass, I sensed that he was a sad man. Sometimes he put me in mind of Mr Hume, the headmaster of the British school. Perhaps, like Mr Hume, he wished he was far away in a distant country. Once, during the lavabo at mass, when I was pouring the water over Père Teilhard's hands, I had a sudden thought. Could it be that he was haunted by the spectre of Peking Man whose bones he had helped to assemble and exhibit in a glass case in the Peking museum?

After mass Père Teilhard always knelt for a long time at the prie-dieu in the sacristy. When I looked at his tall, dignified figure and grave face, I couldn't help thinking of Pat's cartoon of the pathetic knight in the tall black hat.

After I had been serving mass at the chapel of the Jesuits for about a year, Father Superior arranged with my mother that I should help Père Philippe and another of the French priests, Père Joubert, with their English.

Our lessons, which took place once a week in the evenings, were held in the library of the priests' house. They lasted about an hour. Each of the two Fathers would read aloud a passage from *The Life of Matteo Ricci* and I would correct their pronunciation. During our lessons, Father Chou, the Chinese librarian, would hover about in the background, smiling. It was easy to see that the other Fathers wished he would go away.

Father Chou was small and thin, and wore large horn-rimmed spectacles. He never seemed to stop working. After my lessons he would teach me some Chinese history. It was from him that I learned why the moon was so important to the Chinese. Because they travelled by night, the nomads of the Interior had always fixed their calendar by the waxing and waning of the moon. That custom became widespread in China where the moon now governed the dates of all the festivals.

I was leaving the priests' house after my lesson one evening when, ahead of me, I saw the Lama walking slowly down the avenue of ash trees. As he neared the end by the chapel, a figure appeared from behind one of the trees. The Lama stopped as the figure, which was that of a young man, drew near and handed him a piece of paper. For a moment I could see the young man's face. It was A Chin, Y Jieh's son! Amazed, I stood there watching as the Lama slipped the paper into the side pocket of his robe and walked on to the chapel while the young man disappeared in the direction of the gates.

Was it really A Chin that I had seen? And why was he delivering a secret message to the Lama? The questions raced through my mind on the way home.

When I next saw A Chin, he was playing Chinese chess with Pat, late at night. 'Did I see you at the Jesuit college? And did you give something to a priest there?' I asked him. He and Pat laughed and went on playing without answering me. As I was leaving the room, I turned to look at A Chin again. A cloud of smoke from his small pipe curled upwards, covering his face.

□

Walking along my secret path to the Jesuit college one Sunday morning, I suddenly stopped. Ahead the sun was directly behind a slender tree trunk. Together they looked just like the Chinese character for 'east' which Jieh-jieh often drew. A vertical line for the tree trunk, a sweeping branch on either side and the sun behind. I realized with delight that the path was a perfect place for the old game I used to play on my way to the Hidden Creek. After this I would often dawdle on the path, searching for characters in the branches and twigs of the shrubs and in the stones on the ground.

Father Chou, the librarian, was always willing to answer my questions about Chinese characters. He was not surprised to learn how much care Jieh-jieh took of her practice sheets. He told me that, after practising characters, some Chinese would place the used sheets of paper in a special urn in their local pagoda as a mark of respect for the ancient characters. He was impressed, though, when I told him that Jieh-jieh could write out some of the sayings of the Taoists.

'Why did Father Ricci attack the Taoists?' I asked him one day. Father Chou smiled patiently. 'The ancient sayings of the followers of the Tao have a certain wisdom and beauty, but they can be too reckless. They scoff at all government officials and scholars. They even ridicule the idea of obedience to the head of the family. Filial piety, as Confucius taught, is an important virtue. It makes for harmony. Look at the Society of Jesus. We have a Father General in Rome whom we obey. Without that discipline we should break up.'

On my way home from the library, I thought of the Taoist saying, 'Our lives and the whole world around us are changing all the time like the action of a galloping horse.' I stopped now and again to see if I could find anywhere the character for 'horse' with its flowing mane. But it was getting too dark to see easily.

Night was falling. If the universe and everything in it moved like a galloping horse in the day, how did it move at night? Like a tiger, perhaps? A tiger with its belly close to the earth, moving stealthily in the moonlight towards a pool of water screened by rushes.

XII

'Halt! Left turn!' Mr Hardcastle, the Scoutmaster of Number One Troop Tientsin Boy Scouts, called out his orders and we turned to face the cenotaph. 'I want you to be the smartest unit tomorrow,' he said as we began our rehearsal for the Armistice Day parade.

My broad-brimmed cowboy-style hat was much too big for me. I hoped that the chin-strap would keep it from flying away in the wind. The fingers of my right hand holding my scout's pole were numb, and my knees were blue. Was it ever as cold as this in the South African veldt where Colonel Baden-Powell had invented this uniform? It was a good thing that no one from my old school was watching through the park railings. At St Louis we used to make fun of the Boy Scouts. Now I was one myself. The thought made me miserable and I wished I hadn't joined. The trouble was that, unlike Pat, I lacked the courage to say no when Mr Hardcastle asked for recruits.

Suddenly I realized that the rest of the troop had wheeled away to the right, leaving me standing. Mr Hardcastle glared at me as I hurriedly caught up with the others. He said nothing, but I had an uneasy feeling that he could read my disloyal thoughts.

That night was clear and frosty. I knelt on the window seat in our bedroom and looked up at the bright stars. In Ireland and England it was only midday, while here in China it was already eight o'clock at night. Early tomorrow morning people in Europe would see these same stars. It was amazing to think that the light reaching us from the stars had begun to travel towards our planet long ago before the Grand Canal and the Great Wall were built. Thinking about the distant stars made me feel part of a whirling universe of light and darkness. Deep in that reverie I slept.

In the middle of the night we were wakened by the sound of gunfire. The bangs went on for about half an hour and sounded much louder than any guns I had heard before. My mother came into our room, looking pale. 'What is it?' she said. 'It can't be the war-lords. They never attack in the winter.' When she had gone I lay in bed, listening for the guns. The mysterious world of light and dark where my soul moved with the planets and stars had faded like a dream and I was back in Tientsin again, a young boy in a besieged city.

By the time the Armistice Day service started in the morning rumours of what had happened in the night had spread all over the Concession. The ex-emperor Pu Yi had been carried away from Tientsin following a battle.

As yet, only the Japanese High Command knew the full story. Forty men in the pay of Colonel Doihara had crossed from the Japanese Concession into the native quarter where they fired revolvers at the Chinese police. In the battle that followed, Japanese armoured cars also opened fire, killing several people. During all that chaos, which was a planned diversion, Colonel Doihara and three of his officers arrived at the Quiet Garden by car. They disguised Pu Yi in a Japanese officer's overcoat and cap, and drove him into the British Concession along Victoria Road past the cenotaph and down to the ferry on the bund. There the ex-emperor and his escort boarded a motor launch which sped to Taku where a Japanese steamer, the *Kyushu Maru*, awaited them. From Taku they sailed to the port of Dairen in the Japanese-controlled part of Manchuria.

When, later, all this was discovered, people said that you had to admire the 'Lawrence of the East'. His well-timed coup had deprived General Semenov of his rich client and rescued the prisoner of the anti-Ching movement.

Ignorant of most of these events of the night before, the British community continued their traditional service of remembrance.

> 'O God, our help in ages past,
> Our hope for years to come,
> Our shelter from the stormy blast. . . .'

The sad, quavering voices rose and fell. Two members of the British Legion, looking much older than they had done the previous year, laid the last wreath at the foot of the cenotaph. People wiped away their tears and shuffled their feet to keep warm. The Japanese officers grasped the hilts of their long swords and looked on impassively.

The first snowflakes of winter were falling as the pipers of the Argyll and Sutherland Highlanders, whom the exiled Pu Yi had admired so much, played their lament, 'The Flowers of the Forest'.

In the weeks following Armistice Day 1931 the Japanese began to pour more and more troops into Manchuria. The Prime Minister of Japan, General Tanaka, issued a brief statement to the world: 'The Japanese army will ensure that peace reigns over Manchuria.'

This news, however, was received with dismay in Tientsin. It was one thing for the Japanese to punish the bandits who harassed their concessions in southern Manchuria, but quite another for them to occupy the entire province. Many an anxious resident must have been reassured by the firm words of Woodhead. 'It is Japan's duty to keep the peace in the Far East,' he wrote in a special article. 'After constant provocation by the Chinese, Japan has at last hit back. We should be grateful that she, alone of the allies, has staved off the final surrender of foreign rights. Thanks to General Tanaka's positive China policy, the abolition of extra-territoriality is now in cold storage.'

The Chinese government protested to the League of Nations in Geneva about the invasion. But without American support the League was unable to take effective measures against Japan and merely announced that a commission would be sent to investigate the affair.

The President of the League of Nations was mentioned in the newspapers nearly every day. He was Mr de Valera, a name I had not heard since Brother Faust and my father used to shout 'Up Dev!' at the end of their parties in our drawing-room. To my amazement, Mad Mac told me that the same de Valera, the rebel leader of the Easter Rising in Ireland who had been sentenced to death by the British, was now president of the assembly of so many important nations.

While the League of Nations commission deliberated, the Japanese invasion continued. By the beginning of 1933 every Manchurian town, from the Siberian border in the north to the Great Wall in the south, was under the flag of the Rising Sun.

□

On the first day of March, 1934, the frail figure of Pu Yi, dressed in the imperial state robes of the Ching family, stood before an altar in the eastern outskirts of Chang Chun, Town of Eternal Spring. A red sun had just risen over the surrounding mountains and forests and was spreading a reluctant glow on the frosty Manchurian plain when Pu Yi began to carry out an ancient ritual. The liturgy was a simple one: the burning of the incense, the brief Address to Heaven, a bow to the altar and the red sun behind it and Pu Yi was Emperor of Manchuria.

Later, sitting in an open motor-car, Pu Yi was driven along the few roads of Chang Chun to be shown to his people. Outside his palace, edicts proclaiming the new Manchurian Empire were read. Some obedient cheering came from the Koreans and Japanese in the streets, but few Chinese joined in. Already they were calling Pu Yi the Puppet Emperor.

Woodhead, who had been a guest of honour at the coronation ceremonies, wrote an account of them for his old paper. He ended it on a wistful note. 'Before I left Manchuria,' wrote Woodhead, 'the Emperor granted me the honour of a private audience. He asked after Tientsin. I assured him that all was well there. Then, as we shook hands, the Emperor told me how much he missed all his British friends, especially the members of the St Andrew's Society.'

The social round in the British Concession followed its usual course in the winter of 1934, with dinner dances at the Country Club, the ice carnival at the skating rink and concerts at Gordon Hall. The St Andrew's Day ball in the Astor House Hotel, an occasion which Pu Yi used to grace with his presence, had a special tinge of nostalgia that year. When the orchestra, led by Herr Schneider, played the highland lament 'Will Ye No Come Back Again?' in a slow and melancholy foxtrot time, many of the dancers in the tartan-decorated ballroom must have thought of the young emperor across the Great Wall.

'Should auld acquaintance be forgot
And never brought to mind?
We'll tak a cup o' kindness yet,
For auld lang syne.'

The words of the parting song died away. Outside in the pitch
darkness one or two Chinese passed by on their bicycles. A
policeman walked up and down his beat near the cenotaph.
Then the front doors of the hotel opened and people streamed
out into Victoria Road, laughing and calling out, 'Good night.'

The noise of car doors slamming and engines roaring
disturbed the crows nesting in the trees bordering the park.
Some of them took off and flew about cawing before settling
down in their tree tops again.

□

In the depths of the winter a dark cloud appeared on Tientsin's
horizon. Reports began coming in of a large horde of refugee
peasants who were making their way there from Manchuria. In
twos and threes at first, then in bigger groups, they infiltrated
the Russian Park with desperate skill. As fast as the police could
round them up they came on relentlessly like a swarm of locusts.
They crossed the frozen river in sleighs and climbed up the bank
onto the British bund. Hundreds of them were arrested, but
some managed to slip through the cordon of troops and
disappear down Taku Road and the small back-streets. The
Watch Committee appealed to residents to report anyone they
might suspect of harbouring the peasants or guiding them to
secret hide-outs.

Hearing someone talking Russian in an agitated voice in our
backyard one day, I looked out of the window and was surprised
to see Nikitin there with Pat and Jieh-jieh.

'A Chin . . . there's been an accident,' Pat called up to me.
Then he turned and ran down the back alley. I tore after him
down Elgin Avenue into Racecourse Road. A small crowd was
standing outside the railings of the Jesuit college. Two
policemen and an inspector were keeping people back from a
body lying face downwards in the roadway. A piece of sacking
covered its head and shoulders. One limp hand was touching the

ground. I did not need to see the tobacco stains on the fingers to know that the hand was A Chin's.

'Knocked down by a car,' the inspector said to Pat. 'The driver did not stop. You know the dead man?' He drew the sacking back.

I walked away full of thoughts of my father lying in the roadway in Shanghai. It was only afterwards at home that I realized with a shock that I had not thought of A Chin at all, but only of my father. Why, I could not say.

I did not see Y Jieh or Jieh-jieh weep after A Chin was killed. They took one day off to bury him. That was all.

□

On the first fine day of spring when the ice on the river was breaking up, Captain and Mrs O'Riordan invited us to tiffin. Afterwards we were to go with them to the Astor House Hotel to watch the Argyll and Sutherland Highlanders, whose tour of duty was over, march out of Tientsin.

The O'Riordans lived in a small house near the British army barracks. On their front gate was the name 'Blackrock'. Mrs O'Riordan opened the front door and, with a sad smile, said, 'Welcome to our little corner of Dublin.'

In the sitting-room a coal fire was burning in a small grate surrounded by blue and white tiles. The portly figure of the Captain, in brown tweed suit and regimental tie, stood in front of the fire. His hair had become much greyer in the last year. On the walls were prints of old Dublin: Trinity College, St Patrick's Cathedral and the Castle. After he had given my mother a gin and lime, the Captain returned to the fireplace, squared his shoulders and, with a glass of whiskey in his hand, started to address us on the state of North China. While he was talking, Mrs O'Riordan kept leaving the room to see if tiffin was ready. Each time she returned, the Captain, his face flushed with annoyance, would wait until she had slipped nervously into her armchair before finishing his sentence.

'You've got to hand it to the Japs,' said the Captain. 'Always one move ahead. They're nothing if not businesslike. Look how they are managing in Manchuria. No more bandit raids on the trains now.' He downed the remains of his drink and walked over to a side-table to refill his glass.

'It's very worrying, the fighting in the south. . .,' my mother said. Pat's eyes searched the doors and windows, looking for a way of escape.

'All I can say is that the Russians are behind it all,' said the Captain, on his way back to the fireplace. 'Did you know, Grace, that the Chinese Reds decorate their meeting-rooms with portraits of Marx, Engels, Lenin and Stalin? Oh, they take their orders from Moscow all right!'

This talk about the Russians only made my mother more worried. Like most people in Tientsin, she had been led to believe that the Chinese communists in the south were but a few bandit gangs. Now they were being spoken of as the Red Army. The tune had been changed in an alarming way.

The Red Army had always drawn its support from the industrial workers in the southern towns. It had few links with the peasants. But, after a recent defeat by Chiang Kai Shek's Nationalists, the Reds had been forced to seek refuge in the countryside where, for the first time, they began to enlist peasants. Stalin himself gave his approval to this change of tactics by decreeing that the Chinese communists must harness millions of peasants in the service of the revolution.

Harried by Chiang Kai Shek's forces, the Red Army retreated to the mountains in the south, where they regrouped. We did not know this at the time, but, even as Captain O'Riordan was lecturing us in his sitting-room, the Red Army had already begun its long march northwards.

'Just like the Chinese,' the Captain went on. 'One lot of revolutionaries in the south talking of a new communist China; another lot in the north led by members of an ancient secret society who want to put the clock back five hundred years to the time when there was a peasant emperor. Well, Reds or White Lotus, if either lot try to start something up here in the north, they'll be wiped out. Shall I tell you why?' The Captain paused. No one dared to move. At last he let out his military secret. 'Bomber aircraft! That's the answer. The Japs have squadrons of them ready for action. Bomber aircraft. You mark my words. Warfare will never be the same again.'

Mrs O'Riordan tiptoed out of the room. A burning coal fell through the bars of the grate. I watched it dulling. Then another fell, and another. I had seen some Japanese bomber aircraft landing by the racecourse a few weeks before. Looking deceptively frail, they hovered in the air like dragonflies, their double wings marked with the red sun. Then, one after the other, they swooped down to the ground, swaying as they trundled along.

The sound of someone laughing startled me. I looked up. Everyone had gone into the dining-room. 'There he goes, dreaming again.' The Captain was holding the door open for me. 'You've been left at the post, Brian.' 'Sorry,' I mumbled as I hurried to join the rest of the party.

After tiffin we all squeezed into the Captain's car and drove to the Astor House Hotel where we were to watch the parade from the verandah. As soon as we got out of the car I noticed that Pat had vanished. How on earth had he done it? I never found out. Pat was not one for giving away his tricks.

Soon we heard the drums and pipes of the Argylls leading the regiment along Meadows Road towards the cenotaph. Mr Peebles and members of the British Municipal Council came out of the Gordon Hall and stood talking on the steps. Near them I could see some members of the British school staff.

Just then a group of Japanese officers in riding boots and spurs and carrying long swords, arrived at Gordon Hall to take part in the farewell. They saluted Mr Peebles, who lifted his top hat and bowed to them. There was a buzz of excitement among the British spectators and some of them peered at the Japanese officers to see if the Lawrence of the East was among them.

The Argylls wheeled into Victoria Road and marched by the hotel. In their tour of duty they had not been called on to do any fighting after all. When they reached home many of them would retire to the towns and glens of Scotland. What memories of Tientsin would they take with them? The long and bitter winters, perhaps, when the north winds from Siberia covered the ice with dust. Or the summers when stray dogs roamed the streets and flies were everywhere.

Chains of small crackers began to explode, sending up a cloud of angry blue smoke as the Argylls neared Gordon Hall. They passed under the paper arch with its sad message 'Farewell the Argylls'. Miss Hamilton of the Scottish bakery was in tears. 'Eyes left!' roared the colonel of the Argylls, and Mr Peebles took off his hat and held it across his heart as he received the salute.

One person who would have loved to have been at the saluting base was missing from this scene. Pu Yi sat in his palace in Manchuria seeking what consolation he could from his Buddhist devotional books. Would he ever, as he had once dreamed, fashion his own tartan or have his own pipe band?

The last crackers banged and spluttered. Now we could hear the drums and pipes again, and we had a last sight of the marching column through the thinning cloud of smoke.

> 'Will ye no come back again?
> Will ye no come back again?
> Better loved ye canna be
> Will ye no come back again?'

Everyone began to move away, but Wang the park policeman still stood to attention, staring after the Highlanders. The strange sound of their bagpipes always left him bewildered. It was a sound he would never hear again.

XIII

Every year on the 5th of November Miss Wright organized a bonfire and fireworks display in the school playground. As well as giving the school a treat, her object was to provide a touch of Guy Fawkes Day atmosphere for those of us who had never been to England. Miss Wright made the straw guy herself. It was lashed to a piece of wood and propped up on top of the bonfire. At the climax of the evening she would ask the headmaster to light the bonfire.

Hiding at the back of the noisy crowd, all celebrating the defeat of the Catholic plot against King James, I felt like a spy. In England they burned an effigy of the pope as well as a guy. Miss Wright would like to do the same thing here, I thought in mounting excitement. I had better be careful. Supposing she found out the meaning of the Jesuit code A.M.D.G. on my essays? Perhaps she knew already!

I slunk off into the dark before the end of the ritual. Away from the cheering and the bangs, I felt braver. What if Guy Fawkes had blown up the Houses of Parliament? I wished he hadn't been caught. This daring thought made me forget how cold and dark it was as I trudged along Avon Road on my way home.

For Miss Wright, the golden age of the world was that of King James I of England. The Tudors who went before and the Hanoverians who followed were of little significance. Luckily for Shakespeare, he had lived on into the reign of King James. Miss Wright read us passages from his plays in her metallic voice. We also took it in turns to recite the different parts. I found the readings boring, but what was even more tedious was the task of learning passages of Shakespeare for our examinations.

171

On Speech Day, after the community singing, the head-master's address and the prize-giving, the pupils performed one of Shakespeare's plays. We always had the play which was the subject for the school certificate examination. Mr Hume said it was an honour to be given a part. Miss Wright selected the players, directed the play and sat in the wings acting as prompter. Speech Day was long and tiring. By the time the play had dragged to its end, you could see some of the parents yawning. Once, during *The Merchant of Venice*, Miss Wright prompted Shylock so loudly that the audience was startled. I felt sure that she had done it on purpose because she had seen someone asleep.

In 1935, when it had looked like going on forever, Miss Wright's reign suddenly came to an end. She announced curtly one day that a new member of the staff, Miss Mackintosh, would be taking our English classes.

Mr Hume swept into our classroom, his gown flowing like the wings of a giant bat. Behind him walked a shy young woman with blue eyes and pink cheeks. She had just come to us from St Andrews University in Scotland. Mr Hume introduced her and departed, leaving Mary Mackintosh standing before us, looking radiantly beautiful. Under her gown she wore a white blouse and a tartan skirt. Her long chestnut-coloured hair fell down below the collar of her blouse and touched her shoulders. There was a wistful smile on her face as she contemplated the prison where she was destined to spend so many hours. I pictured her leaning over the ramparts of a castle, looking down on the blue waters of a loch the same colour as her eyes. Around the loch, purple heather covered the hill slopes where she longed to roam free. She was Mary, Queen of Scots! The castle was Gordon Hall, where she had been imprisoned by Miss Wright acting as Queen Elizabeth and by Mr Hume as Archbishop of Canterbury. 'Who will rescue me?' Mary's eyes seemed to be pleading.

Shakespeare was no longer boring. The play for this year was *Twelfth Night*. I couldn't have enough of it, and even took it home to read in the evenings.

It was not Miss Mackintosh's beauty alone that captivated me, it was her soul. When I dreamed during a lesson, she did not trap me and bring me back to earth with a question. Perhaps she was a dreamer herself, I thought. Sometimes, in the middle of our recitations, she seemed to be far away in another land.

'Your brother Pat has got a part in the school play.' A chorus of voices greeted me when I entered my classroom one day.

'I don't believe it.'

'Go and see for yourself.'

At the break I walked down the corridor to the school noticeboard. The cast for *Twelfth Night* was pinned to it. Glancing down the list of characters, I came to 'Feste, a fool. . . Patrick Power.'

So it was true. How daring of Miss Mackintosh to choose Pat! Mr Hume would not be pleased. This term alone, Pat had twice been caught smoking in the playground. He had played truant again, and worst of all he had been caught drawing cartoons of members of the staff during Miss Ransom's still-life drawing class. Everyone knew that he was the most caned boy in the school.

Miss Mackintosh's choice was not only daring, it was brilliant. The more I thought about it, the more I realized how perfect Pat was for the part. Feste, the Lord of Misrule and Master of the Revels, was also the wayward clown who sang those strange and wistful songs. Like Feste, Pat was always poking fun at people in his cartoons. There was also something sinister about Feste, I thought; something which put me in mind of the story-teller in the market-place in Tientsin who ridiculed the scholars and suddenly changed the laughter of the crowd to an uneasy silence.

My mother was delighted when she heard the news. A part in the play might help Pat to settle down, she hoped. Eagerly, she began to compose the music for his songs and, with Y Jieh's help, she set to work making his clown's costume of red and green with a cap to match.

> 'I am gone, sir, and anon, sir,
> I'll be with you again;
> In a trice, like to the old Vice,
> Your need to sustain. . . .'

I sat in the drawing-room, listening to my mother taking Pat through one of Feste's songs. It could have been the story of Pat's life. Recently he had been more elusive than ever. Sometimes he went out very late at night when he thought I was asleep. I said nothing to him about it, but I had made up my mind to find out his secret.

'Do you think you'll learn your lines in time?' I asked Pat a week before the dress rehearsal.

'No, but I can always make them up as I go along,' he said with a laugh.

'I'm sure you will. Do you know how lucky you are to be playing Feste? Miss Mackintosh says the best lines in Shakespeare's plays were given to the fools because they have the wisest thoughts.'

'You seem to know a lot about Shakespeare. You've changed, Brian. You used to hate everything to do with school, but now I'm sure you are going to pass your exams easily. I am never going to take any.'

Pat's words hurt. I knew what he meant. I had not played truant with him for a long time. Even in the evenings after school I stayed at home to work instead of going fishing with him as I used to. Yes, I had changed. The thought saddened me. A few weeks earlier Mr Hume had talked to me in his study. 'Your mother has set her heart on you going on to a university in England,' he said. 'I'm sure you have it in you, if only you will work. Don't you think you owe it to her?'

All the way home that day I had thought of my mother. For her, as Captain O'Riordan used to say, life was a ladder to be climbed. A university degree was one of the top rungs. If one of her children could attain it, how proud she would be. She became obsessed with the idea and would say to anyone who came to the house, 'Brian is going to a university in England.'

One Sunday afternoon I met Père Teilhard and Père Philippe as they were leaving our house after tea. 'I hear you are going to continue your studies in England,' said Père Teilhard. 'It will do you good to see a little of the world.'

Two days before the dress rehearsal Pat was in trouble again. David White, the school's champion athlete, had lost a complete set of cigarette cards, all Hollywood film stars, while playing beedka in the playground. He claimed that he had been cheated by a small gang of whom Pat was the ringleader. Major White of the American Marines had written a letter of complaint to the headmaster. We were all very anxious. With any luck it would take Mr Hume a few days to interview all the gang. I prayed that Pat could survive until Speech Day.

At the dress rehearsal Pat was magnificent. He skipped some lines, put in a few of his own and strolled about the stage as if it was his natural habitat.

The last scene neared its end. My mother's music was played on the school piano. While the lords and ladies, priests, officers and attendants stood listening, Pat sang:

> 'When that I was and a little tiny boy,
> With hey, ho, the wind and the rain,
> A foolish thing was but a toy,
> For the rain it raineth every day.'

The stage darkened, the other players faded away and Pat stepped to the front.

> 'But when I came to man's estate,
> With hey, ho, the wind and the rain,
> 'Gainst knaves and thieves men shut their gate,
> For the rain it raineth every day.'

The day after the dress rehearsal disaster struck. During Miss Ransom's drawing class, when he was meant to be drawing a bowl of fruit, Pat was secretly drawing something else. He couldn't resist showing it to his neighbour, who laughed. Swift as a cat, Miss Ransom pounced and seized Pat's sketchbook. She gasped with horror when she saw what he had drawn. A naked woman knelt before a man seated on a throne. She was offering him a bowl of fruit. He, too, was naked except for a mortarboard on his head. There was no doubt who the two nude figures were: Miss Ransom and Mr Hume. Within an hour Pat was expelled.

'With hey, ho, the wind and the rain. . . .' My mother crashed down on the piano keys in fury. She raged at Pat, the headmaster and Shakespeare in turn. Pat, who had gone into hiding, knew well how to survive these scenes. He would probably be back the next day. I stole past the drawing-room door and slipped downstairs to the basement. Y Jieh and Jiehjieh were sitting on their *kang*, waiting for the storm to subside.

Sung Ge-ge, thinking it would help, began to scratch a sad little tune on his one-string fiddle. But I could hear only Pat's voice as I pictured him standing at the footlights, his cap set at a rakish angle, just before the curtain came down:

> 'But when I came to man's estate,
> With hey, ho, the wind and the rain,
> 'Gainst knaves and thieves men shut their gate,
> For the rain it raineth every day.'

□

In the middle of the night a creaking noise on the staircase woke me up. A half moon was shining into our room. I turned to look at Pat. His bed was empty! Slipping out of bed, I hurriedly dressed and tiptoed down to the backyard. The gate to the alleyway was open.

Now was the time to find out Pat's secret, I thought. I closed the gate behind me as quietly as possible and raced down the alley into Elgin Avenue just in time to see Pat turning into Meadows Road. I kept about two hundred yards behind him as he walked towards our old house on the corner. He turned left at the corner and made for the Hidden Creek.

Once he glanced round, but I froze to the spot and I don't think he saw me. When we were crossing the wasteland I lost sight of him. I kept on until I reached the old bridge. There was not a sign of anyone. Peering down at the murky water, I could see that it was half tide. Suddenly a hand was clamped over my mouth. 'Keep still,' Pat whispered. He took his hand away. 'Did you see any police on the road?'

'No,' I gasped, trying to recover my breath.

'Sit here on the bank and keep a look-out.'

We waited in silence. After a long time I heard the sound of water lapping. The dark shape of a punt appeared from under the bridge. At first I thought it was empty except for the boatman in the stern. Then five people, who had been lying in the shallow hold, raised themselves until I could see their heads and shoulders. They were the same five I had seen roped together in Taku Road that day long ago. A thin man who looked like our old flower pedlar, a boy, two other men and a woman whose face was veiled.

'So they weren't beheaded after all,' I whispered to Pat. He did not answer, but looked straight ahead like a sentry on duty.

The boatman put his passengers ashore on the far bank. Then, steering the punt about, he made for the bridge and disappeared under it.

The five outlaws were climbing up from the water's edge when I noticed a man standing on top of the far bank, waiting for them. It was Mad Mac. For a moment he looked towards us. Then he turned and led the group away.

□

In the autumn of 1935 Pat left Tientsin for Ireland. Our Uncle Jim, who had retired from the Royal Navy and was living near Cork, had offered to find Pat some work there.

It had all been arranged so quickly that when my mother and I waved goodbye to him at the station, it had still not fully dawned on me that he was leaving us for good. As the midnight train steamed out of Tientsin on its way to Manchuria and the Trans-Siberian line, Pat, looking very dashing in his smartest suit, stood at a carriage window. He gave us a carefree smile. Then he was lost to sight.

The red lantern on the back of Pat's train dwindled in the distance, and my mother and I made our way back along the platform and across the wooden bridge. 'He's just like his father,' she kept repeating all the way home in the rickshaw. At the cenotaph we turned into Meadows Road and soon came to our old house. Somewhere down there, beyond the wasteland, was Pat's favourite haunt, the Hidden Creek. Was it only a dream, I wondered, or was it true that he had been a look-out for the Lotus? Would I ever see him again? With any luck I might find him sitting on an Irish river bank, fishing. He would smile and wave and then, such was his magical gift for vanishing, the next moment he would be gone.

In the morning Y Jieh brought me a parcel. 'Pat asked me to give this to you today,' she said. I unwrapped the paper and opened the lid of the cardboard box. Cigarette cards! Hundreds of them! There were British, American, Japanese and Chinese ones. Film stars, famous ships, soldiers of famous regiments, insects and old Chinese stories. It was Pat's complete collection, the fruit of many hours of playing beedka. Inside the box was a note: 'Brian. If you don't want any of these, Kravchuk and Nakvasin will give you a good price for them. Good luck, Pat.'

□

Père Philippe brought the Father Superior of the Jesuits to tea one Sunday. A tall man with dark eyes and a small black beard, he looked like the portrait of St Ignatius Loyola which hung in the library at the priests' house. I took them in to my mother and then slipped away to go fishing.

That evening my mother was very tearful. She sat beside me on the sofa and told me that she had something important to say to me. 'Father Superior asked me whether I thought you had a vocation for the priesthood.'

'What did you tell him?'

'I said I wasn't sure. You seem to enjoy serving mass there, but you are so young. He said that if you ever considered joining the Jesuit Order they would help to pay for your studies. He also said something about you teaching English there. What do you think?'

'I don't know. I haven't really thought about it before.'

'Well, it's a great honour, of course. But you know I want you to go to a university in England. Afterwards perhaps. . . .'

My mother saw Father Superior two or three more times after this. It was left that I should take my school certificate exams, study in England for four years and then return to Tientsin where the Jesuits would give me a post as a lay teacher. If, later, it was found that I had a vocation for the priesthood, Father Superior would be pleased to help.

Walking along my secret path to the college, I thought about joining the Jesuits. Why did Father Superior think I might become a priest? Had one of the Fathers spoken to him about me? I felt surprised and grateful to have been offered the teaching post. My mother, of course, was delighted about it. 'I don't want you to waste your life like your father and Pat,' she used to say often. The words always hurt. I thought of Pat roaming somewhere in Ireland, and I felt a pang of envy. My life ahead seemed ordained. 'Do your duty come what may.' I could see the glint of approval in Brother Paul's watery eyes when, as a small boy, I had read to the class from a book of moral tales.

Brother Joseph greeted me outside the sacristy with a twinkle in his eye. It was obvious that he knew about the talk of my joining the college. In a few moments he told me all his news.

Père Philippe had gone to Peking for a few days. Father Curator was in a bad temper. Père Teilhard was off to New York soon. He would be away for most of the year.

'Again! I never heard of anyone travel so much as Père Teilhard.'

Brother Joseph laughed. 'There are conferences of scientists going on at institutes all over the world these days.'

We went into the sacristy and I put on my cassock and surplice while Brother Joseph bustled about, getting the priest's things ready. Was it God's will that one day I should put on those green vestments and walk up to the altar to offer the holy sacrifice of the mass?

□

On the last Sunday of May I led the old Lama into the chapel.

'*Introibo ad altare Dei*. . . . I will go in unto the altar of God. Unto God who giveth joy to my youth.' This was the last time I would serve mass before leaving for England the next week. I had passed my exams and had been accepted at King's College, London University. My mother was overjoyed, but I felt nothing and had to try to look pleased when she and Mr Hume congratulated me.

The Lama raised his arms until his hands were level with his shoulders. '*Gloria in excelsis Deo*. . . .' When I returned to Tientsin the first thing I should like to do, I thought, would be to serve the Lama's mass. How was it that this unchanging and timeless rite made me feel so free? As free as I had been on that wonderful day at the Shrine of the Rock.

Standing still, the Lama faced the tabernacle in silence before his last blessing. The mysterious saying of the Taoists came to me: 'The teaching that uses no words is beyond the understanding of all but a few in the world.' This old man from the Kingdom of Snow was one of the few.

After mass I went to say goodbye to the Fathers at their house. 'The next four years will soon pass. Then you will be one of us, a teacher,' Père Philippe said, patting me on the shoulder. Père Joubert, Père Chou and Brother Joseph joined in the laughter.

'We have a small present for you from all of us,' said Père Chou, handing me a stone seal. 'The stone comes from the hills outside Peking.'

Three characters were cut in the seal. 'Do you know what they are?' Père Chou asked.

'The third one is *Shi*, "teacher",' I said.

'Correct! And the others are *Buo*, "poor", which is the origin of your name Power, and *Yòu* which means "wandering". So you see, Poor Wandering Teacher.'

Everyone smiled at my new Chinese name, Buo Yòu Shi.

On my way home, I turned to look through the iron railings at the red brick of the Jesuit college. Some early swallows skimmed along the ground and wheeled above the green of the ash trees. Nothing else stirred. The marshy land beyond the trees and the priests' house was veiled in mist. Was it a hiding place of the secret society of the Lotus? Ever since the day I had seen the figure appear from behind a tree and hand a message to the Lama, I had gone on imagining that this place was linked with a Lotus cell. One day, perhaps, I would know the truth.

□

We were having supper in the backyard when Mad Mac came in to say goodbye to me.

'When I come back from England will you take Y Jieh and me to the Interior?' I asked him.

He laughed. 'Where do you want to go in the Interior? It's a big place.'

'To the edge of the desert where the herds of wild camels are. We could go in a Peking cart.'

'One thing at a time,' said Mad Mac. 'Here you are just off to the other end of the world, and you talk of going to the Gobi. You're as big a wanderer as Pat.'

The others laughed. 'He has a new name now, Poor Wandering Teacher,' Sung Ge-ge said with a grin.

'It's really a joke,' I blushingly explained to Mad Mac. 'The Jesuit Fathers gave me a seal.'

He gripped my arm as if to reassure me. When he left I crossed the backyard with him and watched him walk away down the alley. At the end he turned and looked back for a moment, just as he had done that night at the Hidden Creek.

Was Mad Mac the leader of a Lotus cell? I longed to know,

but I could never bring myself to challenge him. Supposing it was all my dreams and wild imagining? Once I had been on the point of telling him that I knew Pat was his look-out and that A Chin, too, had worked for the Lotus, just to see how he would react. When it came to it, I was tongue-tied and couldn't utter a word. Perhaps he had Y Jieh to thank, for she had taught me to keep silent about the Lotus.

It was a beautiful June night. Y Jieh helped me to lay my mattress on the flat roof. The sky was full of stars and the Milky Way spread over it from north to south. The moon, floating like a lantern in the eastern sky, was on the wane. Somewhere in the heart of Asia the nomads' caravans would be moving across the desert, bathed in this eerie light.

The great globe of the setting moon had turned to yellow. It was now only just above the balustrade on the edge of the roof. Y Jieh, who was a nomad at heart, believed that one day when the dust from the desert covered everything our planet would become a second moon to light the way for travellers in another world. Although there were fewer nomads now, their way of life had not died out. Many Chinese still lived on sampans which looked as if they had been built for no more than a fleeting voyage through life. Even in a large town like Tientsin the curved eaves on the Chinese houses and pavilions were a reminder of the tents from which they had taken their shape.

I could no longer see the moon. Maybe it was still shining on poor old Nikitin sleeping with an empty bottle beside him somewhere on my secret path. I reminded myself to give him something before I left, as Pat had done. I fell asleep smiling at the thought that soon I should be tracking down Pat by a river bank in the west of Ireland.

□

I had traced the route to England in my old atlas so often that I felt I knew it well. Northwards through Manchuria. Then, at Harbin, westwards into Siberia, circling Mongolia and the Gobi desert. The map showed a mountain chain between the railway line and the Gobi. Sadly, that meant I should not be able to see the great desert. From it came the dust storms of spring, the locusts of autumn and the icy winds of winter. Although we blamed it for all our ills, the invisible and mysterious Interior had always fascinated me.

In Siberia we would skirt the vast Lake Baikal and pass through Irkutsk, Novo Sibirsk and Omsk. Across the Ural mountains into Europe. Moscow, the valley of the Volga, Poland, Germany, France and at last, sixteen days after setting off from Tientsin, the English Channel. Tonight I would start on that journey.

Sung Ge-ge was playing his fiddle in the backyard while Jieh-jieh packed the remains of our supper, bowsers, in a wicker basket which was to be my hamper for the journey. It had B. POWER, LONDON painted in black on the outside. Inside were two bottles of Camp coffee, a tin of golden syrup, a tin of ham and a knife, fork and spoon. I was to buy milk, cheese and bread at the stops on the Trans-Siberian line.

'As soon as I come back I'll take you to Shanhaikwan, Y Jieh.' She smiled and told Sung Ge-ge to go and find two rickshaws, one for my mother, the other for me and my suitcase and hamper. Captain O'Riordan had offered to drive us to the station, but we had refused because it would have meant keeping him up so late.

My mother was very excited. She kept making me check that I had my passport, book of railway tickets, twenty Chinese dollars and twenty English pounds.

Y Jieh came to the front gate with me. She reached out, took my face in her two rough hands and pressed them firmly against my cheeks as if it would help her to remember the shape of my face. It was then that I had my first misgiving. What if I was never to see her again?

'*Zai jian* . . . until our next meeting, Y Jieh,' I said, trying to sound casual.

'Don't forget to buy some apples at Changli,' she said.

The rickshaw coolies moved off at a walking pace and then broke into a slow run. Half-way along our road I looked back. I could just make out Y Jieh's white hair against the dark leaves of the lilac tree. Then we turned the corner.

There was a light on in the drawing-room of our old house in Meadows Road. The umbrella tree, which used to give shade to the pedlars, seemed smaller than I remembered it. We crossed Taku Road. A solitary cart drawn by a mule was trundling along towards the market-place. Our coolies padded around Victoria Park and turned left at the pale grey cenotaph where all was silent except for the sound of a tug's hooter coming from down-river.

Gordon Hall loomed up. All these years and I had never lost the feeling that it was haunted! My mother had not mentioned Yellow Lotus for ages, I thought with relief. She seemed to have forgotten all about her and her terrible threat against the foreigners. Little by little, this town which she used to fear and hate had become my mother's whole world. 'No, I couldn't leave Tientsin, not now,' she had said a short while before when I asked her if she would like to go back to England.

After running through the French Concession, our rickshaw coolies slowed down to walk over the hump-backed Austrian bridge. Another five minutes and we were at the railway station. My mother paid the coolies and we crossed the wooden bridge to the far platform.

Just before midnight we heard the wail of the train's whistle. A pin-point of light in the distance grew larger until the engine pulling the Trans-Siberian train came hissing and clanking into the station.

I found a seat in a third-class carriage, put my suitcase and hamper up on the rack and then returned to the platform.

'You will try and find Pat as soon as you go to Ireland, won't you? And write and tell me how he is?' my mother asked. I promised. The station-master began ringing his handbell. I kissed my mother and climbed up the three steps of the carriage. As the train moved slowly, jerked and then moved again, she waved to me shyly. The pale white oval of her face looked like the face I had seen long ago in the mirror of her bedroom, puzzled and sad. The face became smaller and smaller until I lost it in the crowd waving on the platform.

The train pulled away, giving a long wail on its whistle and drowning the sound of the bell. From my carriage window I could see some lights in the Italian Concession and, a little later, the faint outline of the trees in the Russian Park. We came to the flat country north of the Sea River where, lit by flashes of fire from our engine, the tall silent ranks of gaoliang waited. Reluctantly they let us pass. And then I knew that I had left the Ford of Heaven.

EPILOGUE

The sky over London was the same leaden grey colour as the roadway. A relentless drizzle fell on the rush-hour traffic grinding slowly along Whitehall. The bus window kept misting over and I had to wipe it to see out. We were running late. Big Ben had already chimed nine when we came to the Cenotaph.

1914–1918
THE GLORIOUS DEAD

Peering through the window at the familiar inscription, I thought of that other pale stone monument far away in Victoria Park, Tientsin. It must be five o'clock in the evening there and Wang the park policeman would be getting ready to lock the gates.

I took my mother's letter out of my pocket. The stamp on the envelope showed a junk sailing on a river. For the second time that morning I read: 'The Japanese are closing in on Peking. Their planes bombed Shanghai last week. Hundreds of people were killed on the riverside. Captain O'Riordan says there is no need to worry, but I can't help feeling. . . .' I remembered the Captain standing in front of his fireplace with a glass of whiskey in his hand as he proudly revealed his military secret. 'Warfare will never be the same again. Shall I tell you why? Bomber aircraft!. . .' All modern armies were equipped with that weapon of blind destruction. And they were prepared to use it. Not only over Chinese towns and villages, but over the Basque town of Guernica airmen had rained down bombs on victims they could not see.

184

Once they had taken Peking, the Japanese advanced rapidly to occupy other parts of northern China. The only resistance they met was in the Interior where they were harried by Mao Tse Tung's Red guerrillas supported by the peasant militia. As for Tientsin, the Japanese were its virtual masters now. Accusing the British authorities of 'harbouring anti-Japanese elements', they barricaded the Concession's exits. Those residents who dared to come and go were subjected to humiliating searches.

'These have been terrible days,' my mother wrote in the last letter that reached me from China. 'First the Can Do's left, then the East Surreys. When they marched off to the station there was no band, no crackers, nothing. On the same evening HMS *Hollyhock* sailed away for good. The last British regiment and the last gunboat. I can hardly believe it. They say the Japanese might march into the Concession at any time. The O'Riordans are leaving by ship tomorrow. They wanted me to go with them, but I can't. Thank God Y Jieh is with me. She is the only one I've got now. . . .'

War broke out in Europe. In February 1940, the year I should have returned to China, I was posted to an Irish regiment in the British Army with the rank of second lieutenant.

In December of the following year came Japan's air attack on Pearl Harbour and her entry into the war on the side of Germany and Italy. A few days later Japanese soldiers hoisted the flag of the Rising Sun over Gordon Hall in Tientsin. So, at last, the British Concession had fallen; not to the war-lords, nor to the peasant outlaws, but to Britain's trusted ally. The remaining British residents, including my mother, were rounded up and sent to a Japanese detention camp in Shantung Province. What had become of Y Jieh? I could only hope that she had made her way back to the boat-people in the canal district.

On 6 August, 1945, the atomic bomb was dropped on Hiroshima. Warfare would never be the same again.

For a long time I heard no more of Tientsin. Then, several years after the war, I came across a fragment of news headed 'Peking Man Mystery'. The Ape-man's bones had not been allowed to rest ever since the scientists had dug them out of the hillside at Choukoutien and put them on display in Peking. In

1941, when the Japanese were invading northern China, the American government and Chiang Kai Shek's nationalists agreed on a plan to transport Peking Man to America. He was smuggled out of Peking in a sealed chest by American marines. They were taking him down the Yangtse River when their ship ran aground. The stranded marines were captured by a Japanese patrol. The chest had then disappeared. The curator of the Palace Museum in Taiwan was of the opinion that Chinese pirates had boarded the vessel when it was left unguarded after the skirmish and carried off the chest. They escaped with it up the Grand Canal to Tientsin where they hid it in one of the ancient riverside cellars.

The years passed. I had one last dream of Tientsin before it faded from me to become just a place coloured yellow on a page of my old atlas. . . .

'A thousand years is as a single day in the sight of heaven.' Intoned in a voice I knew from long ago, the words floated down to me as I climbed the steps of the Light of the Sea pagoda. At the top was a small circular room. A monk in a black robe stood at the window with his back to me. His head was bald. I walked forward three paces to stand behind his shoulder. We looked down on the Sea River winding like a serpent towards the Yellow Sea. I could make out the ferry pier quite clearly.

'You are keeping watch?' He did not answer me nor did he move.

Clusters of red balloons decorated the sides of the road below us. A victory parade of soldiers came marching by. They wore green uniforms with red stars on their caps. At the front two soldiers carried a large picture of Mao Tse Tung.

'Will Mao Tse Tung be the new emperor of the peasants?'

The monk remained as silent as the Lama at mass.

It was time to go. I had just reached the doorway when he turned round to face me. It was the old flower pedlar.

'May I come back to the Ford of Heaven one day?' I pleaded. He did not reply, but his eyes were full of kindness, as if he was giving me his blessing. Then he turned back to the window.

□

30 April, 1973

Although it was only eight o'clock when the train from Shanghai reached Tientsin, the square outside the station, which used to be full of rickshaw coolies clamouring for passengers, was strangely quiet. Under the austere regime of Mao Tse Tung few people went out at night for they started work very early in the morning. There were no motor-cars and no street lighting. Only the moon shone on the buildings, bathing them in a soft light.

What an age I had been away! Nearly forty years before I had travelled to Europe from this station, not meaning to be gone for more than four years. But war and revolution had made me an exile until now when parts of China were open again to foreigners for brief guided visits.

I had come from England with a group of twenty people. Our itinerary was strict. We would spend just this one night in Tientsin for, with no sights worth seeing, it was merely a convenient stopping place. The next morning we would be on our way to Peking and the climax of our tour.

There was another, more sinister, reason why we were only allowed such a short time in Tientsin. Foreign visitors were not welcome. The Cultural Revolution was raging and there had been outbreaks of fighting in the city. Recently the commissars had denounced the 'outlaw mentality' of the many vagabonds in the peasant militia. When I asked our Chinese guide about the fighting he talked vaguely about 'a few acts of piracy carried out by outlaw elements'. 'Piracy', 'outlaws': how those words brought back the Tientsin of my childhood. The White Lotus! Perhaps it was they who were fighting against the growing number of petty officials who ordered people's lives.

In the dilapidated ballroom of the Astor House Hotel, re-named the Peace Hotel, my fellow tourists gathered for a meeting. I stood at the back while an official in a grey uniform lectured us on Tientsin. After every two or three sentences he would pause to allow an interpreter to translate his words into English. Mechanically, as if he had delivered the same address many times before, the official produced a stream of facts about industrial developments. Oil had been discovered near the coast, he informed us. New housing estates were going up in the former British Concession whose old buildings would soon be pulled down. The warehouses and ramshackle stalls of the market-place had already been razed and a new people's shopping centre was being built there. The foul-smelling creeks which used to flow through Tientsin were no more. They had all been drained and turned into roads.

Avid for more and more information, our group plied the patient official with questions.

'Who decides the rates of pay for factory workers? The Revolutionary Committee or the State?'

'In the spirit of the Cultural Revolution,' replied the smiling official, 'the State lays down broad guidelines and the factory committees then decide the rates.'

'Is it true that after leaving school everyone in China has to spend two years working in the country with the peasants?'

'Yes. Chairman Mao has said: "Learn from the peasants."'

'Have all school exams really been abolished?'

'Yes. Chairman Mao has said that being examined at school is like being ambushed by an enemy.'

'Are Chinese children taught anything about Britain, about the British way of life?'

Unable to listen any more, I slipped away. From the top of the hotel steps I looked across the deserted street which I had known as Victoria Road. Beyond the park I could see the faint outline of the battlements of Gordon Hall. Pu Yi the puppet emperor used to stand here to watch the Scottish highlanders march by to the skirl of their bagpipes. His journeys were over. At the end of the war, when his Japanese masters were defeated, he had been captured by the Russians in Manchuria and later handed over to the communist government in Peking. There, in the grounds of his former palace, he had been given work as a gardener before being promoted to botanist.

All was quiet. I stole down the hotel steps, hoping that no one would follow me. I had gone but a few yards along the pavement when I heard a flapping noise. A squawk followed by more flapping came from one of the trees bordering the park. The crows! So they still nested here. Bemused, I walked slowly along, half expecting to see Wang standing guard by the park railings.

Outside the stately columns of the Tientsin Club where British businessmen used to meet at lunchtime, big Chinese characters on a poster read: 'Serve the People Institute'. It was here that I turned down to the river.

A sampan bearing no lantern sailed out of the darkness. Leaning on the wooden hand-rail at the end of the ferry pier, I watched her tacking against the tide. Was she a pirate? The waning moon over northern China seemed to be in league with the nomads, pirates and smugglers who had always passed this way, for its faint glow both concealed them and gave them enough light to travel by.

I could just make out the square sail of the sampan as, dipping and rising, she made her way in sole command of the river. Was this really the bustling treaty port where I had spent the first eighteen years of my life?

Foreign steamers, tugs and gunboats used to line this riverfront and night and day gangs of coolies, looking from afar like long lines of ants, would carry sacks on their backs from the ships to the godowns. Now that the ships and coolies had disappeared, this silent and deserted place seemed part of ancient China again as the remorseless river flowed past, oblivious of all the invaders who had come and gone.

Running my hand along the wooden rail smoothed through many years of use, I remembered the feel of it from the days when I used to wait for the ferry to take me across the river. There had been times when the ferry could not manage the crossing to the Russian Concession, but Pat would get across somehow even when the river was frozen. Would I ever see him again? During the war he had been reported missing in action in Burma. There was a slim chance that he might turn up one day. I wouldn't put it past him.

'I am gone, sir, and anon, sir.
I'll be with you again. . . .'

'He's just like his father,' my mother used to say. When, after her release from the Japanese camp, she at last returned to England, no one dared to give her the news that Pat, the one she loved best, was missing. Some instinct must have protected her, for she never asked after him. Now she whiled away her time in England thinking and speaking only of Tientsin in its heyday of the 1920s, as if nothing had changed since then. She would talk about my father as if he was still alive and might come walking up the street at any moment with his jacket draped over his shoulder. Yesterday, before leaving Shanghai, I had gone to visit my father's grave only to find that the cemetery had been ploughed up and turned into a field of gaoliang.

I felt sad and lonely. What had possessed me to return? The wound of exile had taken many years to heal. Now it had re-opened and I felt its deep pain again.

A patch of cloud shaped like a bat's wing was spreading over the moon. It was two hours before midnight. The sampan had changed her tack and was sailing slowly towards me. Were her crew coming for their treasure? I gripped the hand-rail. Although I tried to feel at ease, I couldn't, for I knew that down there at the water's edge the relics of Peking Man lay entombed in one of the Ming cellars.

The sampan had closed to within a boat's length of the pier and was broadside on to me. I could make out two shadowy figures. One sat in the stern while the other, who seemed to be keeping a look-out, stood beside the matting which covered the shallow hold.

Something about the look-out man, the cape around his shoulders and the way he stood caught my attention. Then as the sampan drew even nearer I saw that he was leaning on a staff of thick bamboo which he grasped with one hand. Although I could not see his face, I knew at once that he was the travelling story-teller. Many a time when a child I had come under his spell. I remembered how he could change from an old man to a young one and back again simply by the way he stood. Because he hardly ever spoke he was known as the Fool. But I had seen him silence the crowd with a sinister wave of his bamboo staff and the glare in his eyes.

The sampan turned about and her sail filled as she began the long reach back across the river. Her wash lapping against the pier sounded as if someone was knocking at one of the cellar doors below. Was he trying. . .? I shivered at the thought of that skeleton with its bewildered look. The noise became muffled and died away. 'He was the first being known to have used fire for cooking. . . .' The whispered words of Father Curator floated back to me across the years. What would he and the other Fathers have thought if they could have known that one day Peking Man would end up by this muddy river so close to their museum? The Jesuit college was now a Chinese school. I wondered if I should pay a visit there. Even at this late hour I might find someone from the old days. It was then that I heard wild laughter coming from across the water and I saw the Fool pointing at me as if to say, 'You will never come here again and have only this night left. Why spend it searching for traces of the past? Have you forgotten how to dream?'

The Fool was right. Only things that live in the imagination can last for ever, as his stories had once shown me. But I had been too long in the West and had lost my old habit of reverie. If only I could abandon myself, let myself dream again, I might recapture something of the spirit of the Ford of Heaven.

The sampan was lost in darkness now. In the troubled reflections of the moon on the water a procession of people I had known and loved here returned to me: Y Jieh, my Chinese amah; a Tibetan Jesuit priest whom I used to call the Lama; a hunch-backed coolie and a flower pedlar. Few of them had chosen to come to Tientsin. One or two like myself had been born here. Others such as Y Jieh had drifted here like so much refuse from the creeks. She it was who came back to me most vividly of all.

Drawn by the ever-moving river, I found myself once more on that timeless journey when the ghost of old Cheng had taken me in his sampan through a maze of canals and creeks until we reached the estuary of the Sea River. I could see the ruins of the last Taku fort standing against the mudflats. On the eastern horizon a thin strip of dark blue revealed the distant sea.

A woman was cutting rushes on the shore of a small island in the estuary. After a while she knelt to bind the rushes. She wore a blue shirt over her trousers. Her feet were bare. Past her flowed the yellow-brown waters of the Sea River. Everything was coloured brown: the river, the mud houses on the far bank, the few willow trees and the sails of the junks and sampans moving above the line of rushes. Only the woman's blue shirt and the strip of dark blue sea to the east gave a change of colour to the scene.

Wild geese, beginning their long journey to the north, rose up from the salt marshes and flew low over the estuary. Their flight disturbed flocks of rice birds which circled in the air like dark clouds before settling down again.

Hearing the call of the geese and the strong beat of their wings, the woman put down her reaping knife and stood up to watch them. She knew that when they reached the Garden of the Orioles they would turn and fly northwards across the plain to the end of the Great Wall at Shanhaikwan. They and their kind would return many times before the sea became a desert and the dust from the Interior covered everything.

Long after the geese had disappeared beyond the Ford of Heaven she stood looking as if she could see further than the end of the world.